THE MORAL JUSTIFICATION
OF SUICIDE

THE MORAL JUSTIFICATION
OF SUICIDE

By

JERRY JACOBS

Professor of Sociology
Department of Sociology
Syracuse University
Syracuse, New York

CHARLES C THOMAS • PUBLISHER
Springfield • Illinois • U.S.A.

Published and Distributed Throughout the World by

CHARLES C THOMAS • PUBLISHER
2600 South First Street
Springfield, Illinois, 62717, U.S.A.

© *1982 by* CHARLES C THOMAS • PUBLISHER

ISBN 0-398-04725-1

Library of Congress Catalog Card Number: 82-5852

With THOMAS BOOKS *careful attention is given to all details of
manufacturing and design. It is the Publisher's desire to present books that
are satisfactory as to their physical qualities and artistic possibilities and
appropriate for their particular use.* THOMAS BOOKS *will be true to those
laws of quality that assure a good name and good will.*

Printed in the United States of America

I-R5-1

Library of Congress Cataloging in Publication Data

Jacobs, Jerry.
The moral justification of suicide.

Bibliography: p.
Includes index.
1. Suicide--Moral and ethical aspects. I. Title.
[DNLM: 1. Suicide--Psychology. HV 6545 J17m]
HV6545.J25 1982   179'.7   82-5852
ISBN 0-398-04725-1   AACR2

PREFACE

HAVING spent the past fifteen years studying and writing about suicide, it recently occurred to me that it might be useful to integrate these collective works into a book. In reviewing these past efforts, I find that I have amassed a tidy little pile of research on the subject. Apart from the book, *Adolescent Suicide,* I have authored chapters in textbooks and numerous articles in professional journals.

These works have, from the beginning, a common thread. They are all concerned in one way or another with the conscious, rational, and moral nature of suicide. This was true at a time when it was much more fashionable to write about the unconscious, irrational, and immoral nature of suicide.

There were two reasons for this. First, sociology, because of the profound influence of Durkheim, did not concern itself much with the intentions, motives, or morals of suicides (or anyone else). Secondly, psychologists and psychiatrists who were interested in the individual, and his intentions, motives, and morals, were not much interested in conscious rational behavior because of the profound influence of Freud.

The works found in this book are novel because they combine a sociological perspective with what has traditionally been a psychological concern. Many have seen the benefit of this marriage.

In the past decade, the arguments contained in these works have convinced many from within the discipline, as well as practitioners of various persuasions. The author hopes that the reader will be able to join these persons in their enthusiasm for the perspective set forth below.

JJ

ACKNOWLEDGMENTS

I THANK the following publishers and journals for giving permission to utilize previously published papers in revised and abridged format:

Jacobs, Jerry: A phenomenological approach to the study of suicide. *Omega, 2*:241-246, 1971.

Jacobs, Jerry: A phenomenological study of suicide notes. *Social Problems, 15*(1):60-72, Summer, 1967. (Reprinted with permission of the *Society for the Study of Social Problems.*)

Jacobs, Jerry: The use of religion in constructing the moral justification of suicide. In Douglas, Jack D. (Ed.): *Deviance and Respectability: The Social Construction of Moral Meanings.* New York, Basic Books Inc., 1970, pp. 229-251.

Jacobs, Jerry: Harry Haller's private sky hook: The role of suicidal ideation in the prolongation of life. *Omega, 3*(2):89-96, 1972.

Jacobs, Jerry, and Glassner, Barry: Manic depression and suicide. *Case Analysis, 2*(1), 1982.

Teichner, Joseph D., and Jacobs, Jerry: Adolescents who attempt suicide: Preliminary findings. *The American Journal of Psychiatry, 122*(11):1248-1257, May, 1966.

Jacobs, Jerry, and Teicher, Joseph D.: Broken homes and social isolation in attempted suicides of adolescents. *The International Journal of Social Psychiatry, 13*(2):139-149, 1967.

Teichner, Joseph D., and Jacobs, Jerry: The physician and the adolescent suicide attempter. *The Journal of School Health, 38* (9):406-415, November, 1966.

Finally, I would like to thank Professor George V. Zito, Department of Sociology, Syracuse University, for his many helpful suggestions.

CONTENTS

THE MORAL JUSTIFICATION
OF SUICIDE

Chapter 1

ON THE NATURE OF MORAL JUSTIFICATIONS AND THEIR RELATIONSHIP TO SUICIDE

Accounts and Disclaimers: Two Key Forms of Moral Justifications

Accounts and *disclaimers* may be seen as subsets of moral justifications that one offers to another in an attempt to neutralize the negative effects, or anticipated effects, of something untoward that one has done. The emphasis in the literature has been on accounts and disclaimers being rendered in the name of *impression management* (Goffman, 1959) that is, members invoke these conversational modes in order to convince others nothing unusual has happened or is about to happen (Emerson, 1970). This in turn serves to maintain the ordinary and uneventful flow of events and helps to align one's actions to those of others (Stokes and Hewitt, 1976). Such constructions are in keeping with a symbolic interaction frame of reference (Blumer, 1969). The various kinds and forms of these moral justifications have already received serious attention in the literature (Scott and Lyman, 1968; Hewitt and Stokes, 1975).

The Self Accounting to the Self

These formulations maintain that accounts, disclaimers, and other forms of situated moral justifications are always invoked after something untoward has happened or is about to happen. It is further understood that others are aware (or will become aware) of the untoward event and find it disruptive and/or discrediting to the perpetrator.

3

While they have not previously been viewed as such, these formulations are but specific instances of the general case, i.e. one needs moral justifications not only to placate others, but oneself. For what I have in mind, consider the following: One has done something untoward but it has gone unnoticed. In this case, one does not owe others an excuse or justification, since they are unaware that anything unusual has happened to warrant an account. However, we are aware of what we have done, and must excuse ourself for the potential embarrassment that we have almost caused ourself and/or others. Another example: One may not do anything untoward, but begins thinking bad thoughts. Others are unaware of this, and one has every reason to suppose that they will remain unaware. However, on such occasions, we often feel compelled to invoke internalized accounts or disclaimers, not for others, but for ourselves.

In short, one must *sometimes* invoke moral justifications as a neutralization technique (Sykes and Matza, 1957) for others, in order to save or repair a damaged impression that could otherwise jeopardize present and/or future interactions (Goffman, 1967). However, at such times, one not only provides others with moral justifications, but oneself as well. These two sets of moral justifications, one to others and one to one's self, may be the same or different. While it is true that others have dealt to some extent with the internalization and application of accounts (Scott and Lyman, 1968), they differ in many essential regards from the formulation that follows.

Preliminary Summary

What does the discussion come to so far? It comes to this: when one feels that they have somehow generated trouble or the prospect of trouble for the self, one *always* feels the need to placate oneself, but only *sometimes* feels this need with respect to others. When the need is manifest, one may invoke conversational modes referred to as accounts or disclaimers. However, even then one need not necessarily have an inner dialogue. It sometimes suffices in placating the self to feel (without further reflection or elaboration) that one is right.

Not only are accounts and disclaimers invoked by the self on behalf of the self, but more often than not, they are addressed first to the self and then to others (Cressey, 1953). One's strongest adversary is not a particular or generalized other, but oneself. By the same token, one's potential vulnerability, in the final analysis, lies not so much in what others think of us, as in our self-assessment.

Why the Self Needs Self Accounts

The author will argue that in terms of interactional priorities, one's central concern is to be able to live with oneself. From the traditional symbolic interaction perspective, this is accomplished by one's relative success in living with others. Here the looking-glass self provides that one's assessment of one's self is contingent upon one's assessment of how others see him (Cooley, 1902: 183-84). Perhaps, but then again, we may have the cart before the horse. It may be that the way others see us is contingent upon how successful we are in first convincing ourselves that we have a moral leg to stand on. Indeed, it seems that more often than not we undertake our efforts at impression management in that order. This does not preclude those occasions upon which one convinces oneself in the course of convincing others, or finds a way to convince others in the course of convincing oneself.

Whatever the sequence on any occasion, one's success in providing oneself with appropriate moral justifications seems a necessary precondition to being able to live with ourselves. It is further proposed that if one is unable to live with oneself, it is unlikely that living with others would come easy. In fact, it may prove to be the case that unless we are able to routinely and successfully negotiate the moral correctness of our own thoughts and actions with ourselves, we will be unable to live with ourselves or anyone else, at least for any sustained period of time. Such persons would become prime candidates for suicide (Jacobs, 1971).

Forms of Sociation (Simmel, 1955): An Ideal Type

In this regard, consider the following ideal type: (1) One is unable to successfully manage his impression management with himself or others. (2) One is able to successfully manage his impression management with others, but not himself. (3) One is able to successfully manage his impression management with himself, but not with others. (4) One is able to successfully manage his impression management with himself and others. These options can be represented in a truth table (Table 1-I), which follows:

Table 1-I

Truth Table

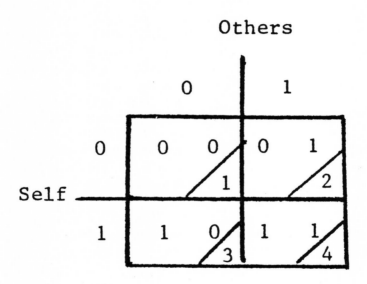

The author will argue throughout this work that human beings generally strive to establish and maintain reciprocal meaningful social relationships with others and that this is a prerequisite to living. Allowing this, which of these four options would be likely to maximize or minimize this prospect?

While in the real world of everyday life, one's relative success in achieving one or another of the above four forms is likely to vary with time and circumstance, we believe that (4) is likely to maximize interactions and (1) to minimize it. Given this, which of the two remaining options would better maximize the prospects of successful sustained interaction: (2) or (3)? We would argue (3), notwithstanding the preference of symbolic interactions and adherents of dramaturgical models for (2). Given the discipline's commitment to the inherent logic of Meadian (Mead, 1936) and Goffmanesque (Goffman, 1959) models, one might ask why?

How the Self Gives Self Accounts

First, consider the following: Much of what is contained in the above four options seems a contradiction in terms. Take the notion of impression management. One manages a presentation of self that one hopes others will accept, but in what sense can one stage one's own self-deception? How can the deceiver and the one being deceived be the same person?

One possible answer is as follows: Just as the successful negotiation of a reputable self is undertaken with others over time with the assistance of accounts and disclaimers, in ways that the developer cannot anticipate in advance — ways that are contingent upon the changing context of the social setting in which the impression management is staged — (one's changing assessment of the situation, the unanticipated introduction of new players or information), one may negotiate with one's self in the same way. That is, one may convince one's self by way of an inner dialogue that one has a moral leg to stand on (and in the process, in no way feel that one has deceived either oneself or others) by the same process that one convinces others of this, in any normal two-party conversation. The problem is not, how could one kid oneself and not know it, but if one succeeded in kidding oneself, how could one possibly recognize it? Allowing that one could succeed through such a process, do we actually provide ourselves with moral justifications in this way? Again, a bit of self-reflection on the reader's part will reveal that one has not far to look for examples and constant reminders that, not only may we succeed in this way, but that we rarely fail.

Having provided that an individual may succeed at his own impression management, it has yet to be demonstrated that option (3) (one is able to successfully manage his impression management with himself, but not others, as in the case of Thomas Moore) would be more likely to sustain a smooth interaction sequence over time than option (2) (one is able to successfully manage one's impression management with others, but not oneself).

After all, the dramaturgical model holds that one need not be convinced of the moral correctness of one's position, but only to convince others of it. Such strategic interactions, if successful, result in the continuation of unruffled interactions within the frame of *nothing unusual is happening*. If unruffled interaction is the goal, then according to the dramaturgical model option (2) would seem to ensure success, while (3) would seem to ensure failure. Notwithstanding the elegance of Goffman's model and its intuitive correctness, it seems not to offer a very good fit with the social reality of natural settings.

Dramaturgy and Social Life

To begin with, people do not usually scheme and plot their impression managements in Machiavellian fashion. Much of what grows in the course of these negotiated realities grows like Topsy; it just grows. Members are in no way sure from the start where they are going or how they might get there in attempting to successfully stage their impression. The whole process, having finally come to whatever it comes to on any one occasion, would leave the participants hard put to reconstruct how it got there, if indeed either is ever convinced of where *there* is in the first place.

In short, life is not a stage and a stage is not life. In life, plays develop within plays where none appear in the script, for the simple reason that in life there is no script. In plays, beginnings are recognizable by the curtain going up and endings by the curtain coming down. Life provides no such convenient way of telling beginnings from endings in interactional sequences. The problem of establishing cause-and-effect relationships in the real world is well documented in the literature. The problem of establishing what is a beginning or ending has more recently carried over into the area of conversational analysis (Schegloff and Sacks, 1974).

A further consideration is that on stage actors act. In life, actors do not recite a playwright's lines in order to develop a plot. Rather, in the course of "playing it by ear" (negotiating reality), one in large measure attempts to construct his own plot. One's success in this undertaking turns upon how well he is able to provide himself and others with appropriate moral justifications for his thoughts and actions.

I do not wish at this time to get involved in an elaborate critique of dramaturgical models or to argue in any drawn-out way about their badness or goodness of fit to the goings-on in everyday life. It is enough, at this point, to note that one has more to do (in order to successfully provide for continued interaction) than to convince others of things that one may or may not be convinced of oneself. This is true even when the things that one tells others are the things they wish to hear in order to hold themselves (and you) in high esteem. Some of the reasons for this will be elaborated upon in the remainder of this chapter.

Impression Management

The role of impression management (within the dramaturgical model) in maintaining social interactions might lead one to wonder: What if, (A) members did not believe what they told others, but others did believe it, and that this was true of conversation in general? Could social interaction be sustained under these conditions and, if so, what forms would it take? Would it bear any resemblance to the forms we all know, or at least talk about as if we did? And what if (B) members always believed what they said, but those hearing it did not? What would the forms of sociation look like then?

The answers to these questions posed by the dramaturgical model, can be found in the answer to the question put earlier, i.e. would ideal type (2) or (3) be better in sustaining successful social interactions? That is, in (B), as in form (3), one successfully manages his own impression management (is convinced of the truth and rightness of his position), but is unsuccessful in his impression management of others (others usually find one and/or what one says suspect). On the other hand, in (A), as in form (2), one is usually successful in one's impression management of others (they find you and what you say credible), but you are unable to manage your own impression management (you are not convinced of the correctness of your own position or action).

Self Accounts as Social Facts

Where and how would one look to find the answer to this question? Here's one possibility. One might do as Durkheim did and treat the matter as a kind of *social fact*. That is, one might look to see if one or the other of these forms of sociation is much more stable and prevalent than the others and constraining upon social behavior (Durkheim, 1964). It could then be argued as Durkheim did that insofar as one found one form to be more stable and widespread in society, it must be performing some essential function in the social order, or it would have atrophied and withered away.

For the author to use this form of argument would be easy. The above formulation has already noted that one more often provides oneself than others with moral justifications when confronted with trouble or the prospect of trouble. Argued in this way, form (3) would be closer to form (4) in providing for the establishment and perpetuation of smooth social interaction or form (2) would be more prevalent. It has been argued earlier that this is unlikely.

We have seen the key role of moral justifications in sustaining social interactions, and what could be more important than this for the maintenance of social structure? In fact, the inability to sustain the smooth flow of interactions on a large scale is referred to in some quarters as *social disorganization.*

While the above argument may appeal to some American mainstream sociologists, it has little appeal to us. Some of the reasons for this can be found in the following pages, as well as in the author's previous writings (Jacobs, 1971).

Living with Yourself: The Basis of Interaction

If the above is not a convincing argument for the superiority of form (3) over form (2), what is? Basically, the above discussion distills itself into the following. Given an either-or situation, would social interaction best be served if one could live well with one's self but not with others, or if one could live well with others but not with one's self? We have seen how living well with one's self is a necessary but not sufficient condition for living well with others. One may live well with one's self and others, or one may live well with one's self but not with others. However, the author has argued that one cannot live well with others without first being able to live well with one's self. The objection will be raised by symbolic interactionists that here we have the cart before the horse. They would insist that one must first learn to live well with others, for to be a social incompetent from the start would mean that one could not develop a self in the first place with which to live well.

An answer to this objection might go as follows. According to Durkheim, society preceded and supercedes the individual and the latter derives from the former, not the other way around. Problem: How could society, however it is defined, precede the individual, when it is itself comprised of individuals? Durkheim deals with the problem of the chicken and the egg in this way. Never mind the day of creation, now or at any point in recorded history; society was there before you were, and you are born into it. Furthermore, things are so arranged, in terms of the distribution of power, that should the individual and society have a disagreement, society is likely to win.

Consider how this argument might be applied to a modified interactionist perspective. Granted that the existence of others precedes and supercedes one's own existence, at some point in time one develops a social self. Let's start there. Indeed, why start any sooner, since prior to the development of the self, we do not have a social being anyway — by definition. Let's start with *social beings* as opposed to *beings*. These are, by definition, persons with developed social selves.

Having arrived at this point and thus disposed of the chicken-and-egg problem, let us now consider if our theoretical social being could keep being social (and keep the social being), if he could live well with himself but not with others, or would it go better for the individual and society if one could live well with others but not with one's self.

As formulated above, it seems that a precondition (but in no way a guarantee) of being able to live well in society is that one must first be able to live well with one's self. It is further postulated that in order to be able to live well with one's self, one must be able to muster moral justifications appropriate to the circumstances that warrant them. Those who cannot will not only have trouble living with others, but quite apart from others' evaluations of them are likely to have trouble living with themselves. Such persons, unable to provide themselves with suitable moral justifications for their own existence, are, as previously indicated, good candidates for suicide. However, even here the process does not stop, since one must provide oneself with a moral justification for suicide as well (Jacobs, 1970; 1967). This point will be more fully developed in Chapters 3 and 4.

In short, one might argue, if everyone were unable to muster appropriate moral justifications for themselves, there would be no social interaction since there would be no one left with which to interact. Viewed in this way, nothing could be more disruptive of social interaction than being unable to live well with one's self, since this now seems to be not only the *necessary but not sufficient condition* for social interaction noted earlier, but a necessary condition for the existence and continuation of social interaction in general.

What about the other way around? Could social interaction exist and perpetuate itself if individuals lived well with others but not themselves (form (2))? It seems not. Indeed, this possibility, while it seemed an intuitively reasonable alternative form of sociation in our earlier discussion, now seems impossible given the above. One could not live well with others, and badly with one's self, because one could not continue living at all in that way, for any sustained period of time. Hence, form (3) in our ideal type is preferable to form (2) because the latter could not exist in principle with any stability over time.

How do we know that those who cannot live well with themselves cannot go on living? The following suicide notes may serve to illustrate the point:

Dear Mom and Dad:

Please forgive *your rotten son* for taking his own life. Don't hate Maria; it's my doing and not hers. *I'm sorry I disgraced you* by doing this but I can't continue to go on without her.

I've been a rotten son to you both, especially you Mom, and I'm sorry. Please forgive me for all the pain and heartache I've caused you. You both were wonderful parents and *you deserved a better son than I was.*

I'm sorry I let you down. *I was a failure* and Maria knew it. Maybe that's why she is leaving me. I did love her though, even though she didn't think I did.

Please forgive me and don't take it too hard. *I never was worth it anyway.* I love you both.

John

(emphasis added)

My darling Maria, *forgive me for all the pain I've caused you. I was an inconsiderate fool and I realize it, now that it's too late.* I honestly loved you my darling even though I didn't show it or tell you. You were a part of me, believe it or not, and I didn't want to face life without you. I needed your time, love, and time for me to adjust and grow up, but you didn't have the patience or nerve to really blow your stack before and put me in my place. I hope I succeed in my plan. *It's not your fault and don't blame yourself.*

I was a fool, a big fool, to gamble with your love. Now this morning you tell me you hate me and it's all over and no chance for me to try and win your love. Well I can't take it and this is the only way out. Perhaps if you marry again and I hope you will, if your next husband goofs as I did for God's sake, if he tells you he's sorry, give him another chance as you couldn't with me. You were so pretty this morning and I longed to hold you, but I know you'll never love me again (if you once did.)

I would have done anything you asked to regain your affection but I don't know how I could have when you wouldn't even give us a chance to try and work it out. I've had my heart broken before as you know and now this! I can't go through it again, Maria, so that's why I've done this thing.

Please forgive me, honey, *I know I was wrong in so many small ways but they kept adding up and you couldn't take it.* I hope I succeed with my plan and that its too late when I'm discovered. I'll always love you Maria darling even if I shouldn't succeed but I hope I do, as it's the only way out.

John

(emphasis added)

My dearest Bob, Marty, and Will,
I am truly sorry.
Please forgive me.
I love you so very much.
Do not blame yourselves.
It is all my fault.
Be good to Mom — she is a
wonderful woman.

All my love

Dad

(emphasis added)

What do these notes have in common? Actually there are many things. For now, it is enough to see that suicides have found it impossible to provide themselves with a moral leg to stand on. They were in short, (as they saw it) their own undoing, and/or responsible for the grief of others they loved.

The reader will see by the conclusion of Chapter 3 the ironic way in which suicides who could not live well with themselves (and others), that is to say, were incapable of providing themselves or others with adequate moral justifications in life, succeed in doing so in suicide notes. Indeed, it will be shown why they had to succeed in such an undertaking at that point in time, in order to bridge the gap between suicidal ideation and suicide.

Conclusions

Accounts and disclaimers are conversational modes that one addresses to others in various forms, and on various situated occasions, in order to *save* or *repair* damaged interactions. However, a more prevalent and important application of these forms of moral justification occur between the individual and himself. The application of the self addressing the self and its need to do so in terms of moral justifications has thus far been a badly neglected topic within the social sciences. I have presented above a general formulation. The rest of the book will, in a variety of ways, demonstrate its specific application to suicide.

REFERENCES

Blumer, Herbert: *Symbolic Interactionism.* Englewood Cliffs, New Jersey, Prentice-Hall, 1969.

Cooley, Charles Horton: *Human Nature and the Social Order.* New York, Scribner, 1902.

Cressey, Donald R.: *Other People's Money.* Glencoe, Illinois, Free Press, 1953.

Durkheim, Emile: *The Rules of Sociological Method.* New York, The Free Press, 1964.

Emerson, Joan P.: Nothing unusual is happening. In Shibutani, Tamotsu (Ed.): *Human Nature and Collective Behavior.* Englewood Cliffs, New Jersey, Prentice-Hall, 1970.

Goffman, Erving: *Presentation of Self in Everyday Life.* New York, Doubleday Anchor, 1959.

Goffman, Erving: *Interaction Ritual.* New York, Doubleday Anchor, 1967.

Hewitt, John P., and Stokes, Randall: Disclaimers. *American Sociological Review, 40*:1-11, February, 1975.

Jacobs, Jerry: A phenomenological study of suicide notes. *Social Problems, 15*:60-72, Summer, 1967.

Jacobs, Jerry: The use of religion in constructing the moral justification of suicide. In Douglas, Jack (Ed.): *Deviance and Respectability: The Social Construction of Moral Meanings.* New York, John Wiley and Sons, 1970.

Jacobs, Jerry: *Adolescent Suicide.* New York, John Wiley and Sons, 1971.

Mead, George Herbert: *Mind, Self and Society.* Chicago, University of Chicago Press, 1936.

Schegloff, Emmanuel, and Sacks, Harvey: Opening up closings. In Turner, Roy (Ed.): *Ethnomethodology.* Baltimore, Penguin Books, 1974.

Scott, Marvin, and Lyman, Stanford M.: Accounts. *American Sociological Review, 33*:46-62, December, 1968.

Simmel, Georg: In Wolff, Kurt H., and Bendix, Reinhard (Eds.): *Conflict and the Web of Group-Affiliations.* New York, The Free Press, 1955.

Stokes, Randall, and Hewitt, John P.: Aligning actions. *American Sociological Review, 41*:838-849, 1976.

Sykes, Gresham, and Matza, David: Techniques of neutralization: Theory of delinquency. *American Sociological Review, 22*:664-670, December, 1957.

Chapter 2

A PHENOMENOLOGICAL APPROACH
TO THE STUDY OF SUICIDE

THE literature on the subject of suicide is both lively and prolific. This is not surprising if we allow that the question of the moral correctness of the taking of life (one's own or another's) is the cornerstone on which the organization and perpetration of society ultimately rests. Basically there are two positions on this question, i.e. suicide may be morally justifiable in some instances, and suicide is never justified. The former position has been well argued by Hume (Hume, 1965), while the latter is found in the theological · discourses of most religions. There are, of course, inherent problems in these philosophical and theological arguments, e.g. the teaching that life is sacred and should be lived at any cost, an evil thought is as wrong as an evil deed, suicide is more sinful than murder, and therefore the contemplation of suicide is a greater sin than murder. This is but one example of the peculiar turns these arguments may take.

While controversies revolving around the moral correctness of suicide still rage, more recently psychiatry and the social and behavioral sciences have tried to concern themselves more with questions of *is* than *ought*. This was seen as a necessary prerequisite for the pursuit of a behavioral or social science. Questions were no longer formulated with respect to whether or not one ought to be able to take one's life (as this would entail a value judgment within disciplines dedicated to a pursuit of a "value free" science) but rather why one wanted to take one's life in the first place, and how, if he succeeded, he was able to do so. Notwithstanding these positivistic pursuits, all classical psychiatric, psychological, and sociological theories of suicide were cast within a suicide prevention framework. Implicit in all of the above was the notion that science had a moral obligation to prevent suicide.

Researchers in the field of suicide (and suicide rates) also sought (in the name of science) to avoid the labels of *philosophizing* and/or *psychologizing* by utilizing one of two basic evasive actions. The first and most successful sociological attempt at this form of scientism (with respect to suicide) was promoted and popularized by Durkheim (Durkheim, 1951). It held that sociology should distinguish itself from and avoid the pitfalls of psychology by eliminating from its purview such considerations as the individual, his intentions, motives, or morals. It was then recommended that having eliminated these *subjective* considerations we further *objectify* our study by eliminating people entirely and treating persons as things. This could be accomplished by studying and interpreting official suicide rates (the data) in such a way as to uncover the external social causal agents responsible for the consistencies found in the rates. These causes would give us an explanation, not only of suicide rates, but ultimately of suicide (Durkheim, 1951, pp. 147-8). Durkheim and others (Gibbs and Martin, 1964; Henry and Short, 1954; Powell, 1950) following in this tradition were led to formulate such questions as to why Protestants consistently kill themselves more than Jews, men more than women, or single persons more than married. The answer to this question was sought not within the individual's psyche, or by a study of his personal circumstances, but rather in the effects of some external social agent upon the groups being considered (Durkheim, 1951, pp. 297-298). Durkheim's argument (having run its course) concluded that it was the relative lack of social integration within varying social groups that explained the rates of suicide within these groups. Apart from the logical inconsistencies one encounters in the development of his argument, Durkheim's promise that an explanation of suicide would follow from the discovery of its causes was never realized. His theory of suicide rates (suicide?) is of no use whatever in anticipating or preventing the suicide of a given individual or group of individuals. For a fuller critique of Durkheim's theoretical — methodological orientation, the reader is referred to the works of Douglas and Jacobs (Douglas, 1967; Jacobs, 1971).

While sociology, with Durkheim's able assistance, sought to establish itself as an independent scientific discipline by pursuing the above brand of positivism, psychology and psychiatry took another tack in attempting to legitimize and expand their influence. Their science was based upon the study of those subjective features Durkheim sought to exclude, i.e. the individual, his intentions, motives, and morals. However, here again, while psychology and psychiatry concentrated upon the actor, they did not concentrate upon his conscious intentional acts, but sought (with respect to the question of suicide) to explain the actor's feelings and behaviors primarily from the orientation of unconscious motivation (Stengel, 1964, p. 45).

> Conscious motives alone cannot adequately explain suicidal acts because only certain people react in this manner to emotional stress. With very few exceptions, there is no situation causing individuals to commit suicide which would not be tolerated by most other people without the emergence of self-destructive impulses. People who tend to react to stressful situations with suicidal acts are called suicide prone.

From this perspective, one's accounts are not taken seriously, i.e. at face value, but are interpreted within a psychoanalytic framework, where the analyst comes to understand the real meaning of the patient's account based upon (a) his familiarity with the psychoanalytical system of explanation and (b) his clinical insight. This kind of analysis frequently takes the following form (Tabachnick, 1957, pp. 167-168):

> . . .It seemed that the most important motive for the suicide was a need for punishment. The patient had been attempting to escape his anger towards his mother for some years; finally, this escape was no longer possible, and it was necessary for him to see that he was angry toward her. He was unable to tolerate this feeling and attempted to deal with it by running away, this time taking a trip to Mexico; yet this was not successful, and *finally he felt hopeless, as if he were left all alone. At this point he made his suicidal attempt.* It would seem that what was really operative here was an attempt to get back into the good graces of his mother by "castrating" himself (by attempting to kill himself), and in this way expiate his guilt (emphasis added).

Those not committed to the analyst's vocabulary of motives (Mills, 1940) cannot help but wonder if it was not the suicide's feeling hopeless and alone (more than his attempt to get back into the good graces of his mother by castrating himself as a way to expiate his guilt) that led to his attempting suicide.

Most psychiatric and psychological explanations of suicide are based upon one or a combination of the following four assumptions, i.e. suicide results from an *unconscious, irrational, maladaptive,* or *impulsive* act. While it is fortunate (in the author's opinion) that psychiatric and psychological explanations of suicide have taken into account the individual and his experiences, it is unfortunate that the four major explanations of suicide noted above have, in conjunction with such notions as frustration-aggression models, broken homes, or the predictive power of psychiatric diagnostic categories, contributed little to our understanding of suicide. Stengel (Stengel, 1964) has noted the following:

> Though none would deny its importance, it must be recognized that statistical data, however interesting, cannot compensate for the ignorance of important aspects of the problem [of suicide] which have so far received comparatively little attention, nor is there yet evidence that psychopathological studies have helped to reduce the suicide rate. Psychopathology has so far been more illuminating with regard to suicidal tendencies as a facet of human behavior than in explaining why suicidal acts occur in certain individuals. The methods of clinical psychiatry have not materially changed since the first studies.

The author has previously presented a detailed critique of the above positions based upon a three-year study of suicides and suicide attempters. The reader will find a more detailed discussion of this study in Chapters 7 and 8. An elaborate discussion of these findings is beyond the scope of this paper. However, a brief outline of some of the study's findings as they relate to psychiatric explanations of suicide may be helpful.

First, the notion that suicide is unconsciously motivated (Stengel, 1964) is difficult to maintain. With respect to suicide this is a difficult position to incorporate. Suicide is defined by Webster as follows: "The act of killing one's self intentionally." The following question arises: How can one unconsciously-intentionally commit an act? Unconscious intentionality seems to the author a contradiction in terms.

Secondly, there is the notion of suicide resulting from an impulsive act (Winn and Halla, 1966; Lourie, 1966; Bergstrand and Otto, 1962). This, too, presents a dilemma given the definition of impulsive. Impulsive is defined by Webster as follows: "a sudden inclination to act, without conscious thought." How can suicide be impulsive if it must be intentional, and intentional implies deliberation or anything intended or planned? Then, too, what of the extensive literature indicating that suicidal persons always tried to communicate their intentions to others in a cry for help? · Once again, suicide as an impulsive act seems to the author a contradiction in terms.

Thirdly, there is a considerable psychiatric literature holding that suicide results from an irrational act (Winn and Halla, 1966; Balser and Masterson, 1959; Maria, 1962). The author and others have taken exception to this point (Jacobs, 1971; Stengel, et al. 1964).

Fourthly, the author's study of the patterning, nature, number, and experience of social-structural events in the lives of suicides and suicide attempters and the way in which suicide attempters and control adolescents sought to deal with their (unwanted and unanticipated) problems leads one to question the notion that suicide and suicide attempts are per se *maladaptive* forms of behavior (Jacobs, 1971).

Finally, broken homes in early childhood do not per se seem to predispose one to suicide or depression in later life — a considerable psychiatric literature to the contrary notwithstanding (Jacobs, 1967). Some of these aspects will be addressed in greater detail in the chapters that follow.

Since Durkheim did not arrive at a theory of suicide and only a very questionable theory of suicide rates (that (a) ignored his own definition of suicide and the importance he attributed to it and (b) underestimated the problems of dealing with official rates in general), and since psychiatric and psychological explanations of suicide based upon the conceptual framework noted above have also proved unsuccessful in predicting or preventing the suicide of any given individual, or reducing the suicide rate, it is perhaps time to reevaluate the merit of existing sociological, psychological, and psychiatric explanations of suicide and to pursue an alternative approach. The approach the author recommends is a phenomenological approach to the study of suicide that seeks its explanation in terms of the individual's conscious, intentional acts.

While this is a rather obvious approach to the study of a problem that is by definition a conscious, intentional act, it is one that has thus far received little attention. Sociological, psychiatric, and psychological studies of suicide have either sought to eliminate the conscious intentions, motives, and morals of the suicide from consideration or to interpret them from within a synthetic framework that does not allow for taking the individual's accounts of his situation and its effects upon him seriously. These two basic positions were traditionally formulated and maintained in the name of either (a) providing a "sociological" formulation of the problem (of suicide) according to the dictates of Durkheim and modern day followers or (b) providing a psychiatric explanation of what otherwise appeared, in terms of a conscious rational choice, to be an "irrational" form of behavior. The author considers the almost universal acceptance of these two positions unfortunate. In the chapter that follows I will take the suicide's accounts at face value and offer an explanation of suicide that is reasonable not *even when* but *especially when* the actor's appraisal of his personal circumstances and their effects upon him are taken seriously (Jacobs, 1971; 1970; 1969; 1967). The analysis is based upon the accounts of suicides and suicide attempters as presented in diaries, letters, and suicide notes or, in the case of the author's study of adolescent suicide attempters, taped personal interviews conducted within forty-eight hours of the attempt. Both sets of suicidal persons noted above were subject to the same processes (one external, one internal). Members of the control group in the adolescent suicide attempt studies were not subject to these processes. The formal features of these two processes will be discussed in some detail in the chapters that follow.

We will begin a more detailed discussion of the points made above with a phenomenological study of suicide notes. The analysis found in this work has the advantage of (1) considering the conscious intentions, motives, and morals of the individual as given by him; (2) taking them seriously; (3) in doing 1 and 2, overcoming (a) the definitional dilemmas previously noted and (b) Mill's dilemma (noted in the forthcoming analysis of suicide notes) by not having to superimpose synthetic and external systems of explanation upon the victim's accounts in order to interpret them; and (4) offering an explanation of suicide that is (a) empirically based, i.e. consistent with the suicide's and the suicide attempter's own accounts of their circumstances where these are accepted *as is*, (b) parsimonious, and (c) internally consistent.

In the author's opinion, the phenomenological approach to suicide given above goes further than traditional sociological, psychiatric, and psychological explanations in helping to understand suicide and better explains the origin and nature of *suicidal ideation*. It offers a formulation that indicates when one is likely to be led to entertain suicide as a course of action and what he must do in order to be able to realize such a plan, having conceived of it. Finally, it is recommended that others utilize the sources of data considered above and analyze the suicide's own accounts within a phenomenological perspective.

REFERENCES

Balser, B.H., and Masterson, J.F.: Suicide in adolescents. *American Journal of Psychiatry, 116*(5):400-404, 1959.

Bergstrand, C.G., and Otto, U.: Suicidal attempts in adolescence and childhood. *Acta Paediatrica, 51*(1):17-26, 1962.

Douglas, Jack D.: *The Social Meanings of Suicide.* Princeton, New Jersey, Princeton University Press, 1967.

Durkheim, Emile: *Suicide: A Study in Sociology.* New York, Free Press, 1951.

Gibbs, Jack P., and Martin, Walter T.: A theory of status integration and its relationship to suicide. *American Sociological Review, 23*(2), April, 1958.

Henry, Andrew F., and Short, James F.: *Suicide and Homicide.* Glencoe, Illinois, The Free Press, 1954.

Hume, David: Of suicide. In MacIntyre, A. (Ed.): *Hume's Ethical Writings.* New York, Collier Books, 1965.

Jacobs, Jerry: *Adolescent Suicide.* New York, Wiley-Interscience, 1971.

Jacobs, Jerry: The use of religion in constructing the moral justification of suicide. In Douglas, Jack (Ed.): *Deviance and Respectability: The Social Construction of Moral Meanings.* New York, Basic Books, 1970.

Jacobs, Jerry: A phenomenological study of suicide notes. *Social Problems,* *15*(1):60-72, Summer, 1967.

Jacobs, Jerry, and Teicher, Joseph D.: Broken homes and social isolation in attempted suicides of adolescents. *International Journal of Social Psy-chiatry, 13*(2), 1967.

Maria, G.: Some considerations apropos of the suicide of minors. *Rassegna Internazionale di Clinica e Terapia* (Napoli), *42*:48-54, 1954.

Mills, C. Wright: Situated actions and vocabularies of motive. *American Sociological Review, 5*(6):904-913, December, 1940.

Powell, Elwin H.: Occupational status and suicide: Toward a redefinition of anomie. *American Sociological Review, 23*:131-139, April, 1950.

Stengel, E., and Cook, Nancy: *Attempted Suicide.* London, Chapman and Hall, Ltd., 1958.

Tabachnick, Norman: Observations on attempted suicide. *Clues to Suicide.* New York, McGraw-Hill Book Co., Inc., 1957, pp. 164-169.

Winn, D., and Halla, R.: *Canadian Psychiatric Association Journal, 11*(suppl.): 283-294, 1966.

Chapter 3
A PHENOMENOLOGICAL STUDY OF SUICIDE NOTES

ACCORDING to Durkheim, the prospect of finding a common denominator in the personal situations of suicides is minimal: "...the circumstances are almost infinite in number which are supposed to cause suicide because they rather frequently accompany it."

In defining the range and effect of personal circumstances on the individual, Durkheim tells us "...some men resist horrible misfortune, while others kill themselves after slight troubles. Moreover, we have shown that those who suffer most are not those who kill themselves most... At least, if it really sometimes occurs that the victim's personal situation is the effective cause of his resolve, such cases are very rare indeed...."

Given the above assumptions, it is not surprising to find out the following: "Accordingly, even those who have ascribed most influence to individual conditions have sought these conditions less in such external incidents than in the intrinsic nature of the person, that is, his biological constitution and the physical concomitants on which it depends."[1]

The author has attempted to categorize a set of suicide notes according to their formal aspects. The perspective adopted is that of the actor, what he must experience, how he must view these experiences, the social constraints restraining him from suicide, how he succeeds in overcoming them, and finally, the precautions he takes to prevent the recurrence of a similar set of circumstances after his death. The paper is based primarily on an analysis of 112 suicide notes of persons who succeeded in suicide in the Los Angeles area. Insights gained by the author through his work with adolescent suicide attempters and their parents also aided in the formulation.

What is most interesting, of course, is that Durkheim abandoned the search for a common denominator to suicide before beginning it. Never having studied a specific case of suicide in detail, indeed at all, so far as I know, how could he know that some resist horrible misfortune, while others kill themselves after slight troubles, that those who suffer most are not those who kill themselves most, or that the victim's personal situation is very rarely the cause of suicide? The author feels that such common-sense assumptions are unwarranted.

There is no need to intuit, as Durkheim has done above, the effects of one's personal situation on suicide. We have available, after all, the best possible authority on the subject — the suicide himself: "I claim that any man who commits suicide of necessity suffers more than any who continues to live. I don't want to die. I cannot make any outsider realize by anything I can write how I have tried to avoid this step. I have tried every subterfuge to fool myself, to kid myself along that life wasn't so bad after all."[2]

The above statement is much more consistent with the position of suicidal persons as related in suicide notes, letters, and diaries than the contentions of Durkheim given above. It is, of course, opposed to what Durkheim believed, since persons do not appear to be killing themselves over arbitrary personal problems or impulsively as in the case of insane suicides. Everyone is forced to kill themselves for the same reason, i.e. they suffer more than anyone who continues to live and are unable, notwithstanding their every effort, to resolve the suffering. In brief, those who suffer most are those who kill themselves most.

The last sentence of Durkheim's concluding statement warrants particular attention as it relates to those who ascribe most influence to individual conditions in seeking an explanation of suicide. Such persons rely primarily upon case history accounts, suicide notes, or interviews with suicidal persons as sources of data. However, even they ". . .sought these conditions less in such external incidents than in the intrinsic nature of the person. . . ."

This has been the general approach of psychiatrists, psychologists, and of some less positivistic sociologists. The reason for this has been that even among those dealing with the individual's personal situation through the study of case histories or suicide notes, they found no common denominator for suicide.

The inability of previous investigators to explain suicide as resulting from a conscious rational process has led them to conclude the necessity of in some way inferring the real meaning of the suicide's story, either by superimposing upon the data an unconscious irrational explanation or some other such synthetic system: "They (suicide notes) strongly suggest the possibility of viewing them as projective devices (in much the same way as MAPS tests or TAT protocols are projective products) from which information may be *inferred* about the subject"[3] (emphasis added).

Psychiatrists also tend to interpret the accounts of their patients from this general perspective. Here the emphasis is on the unconscious, irrational elements, the apparent rational aspects notwithstanding: ". . .suicide is not preeminently a rational act pursued to achieve rational ends, even when it is effected by persons who appear to be eminently rational. Rather, it is a magical act, actuated to achieve irrational, delusional, and illusory ends."[4]

The dilemma confronting those proceeding on the above assumption is well put by C. Wright Mills:

> The quest for "real motives" set over against "mere rationalization" is often informed by a metaphysical view that the "real" motives are in some way biological. Accompanying such quests for something more real and back of rationalization is the view held by many sociologists that language is an external manifestation or concomitant of something prior, more genuine, and "deep" in the individual. "Real attitudes" versus "mere verbalization" or "opinion" implies that at best we only infer from his language what "really" is the individual's attitude or motive.
>
> Now what could we possibly so infer? Of precisely what is verbalization symptomatic? We cannot infer physiological processes from lingual phenomena. All we can infer and empirically check is another verbalization of the agent's which we believe was orienting and controlling behavior at the time the act was performed. The only social items that can "lie deeper" are other lingual forms. The "Real Attitude or Motive" is not something different in kind from the verbalization of the "opinion." They turn out to be only relatively and temporally different.[5]

The author feels that in order to overcome this telling criticism it is necessary to offer an explanation of suicide that is both derived from and validated by some empirical referent. I feel the life situations of suicides as related by them in suicide notes offer such a potential. I will seek to establish the common denominator of suicide in the formal aspects of a process, rather than in some independent event such as a childhood trauma or a later precipitating cause.

Suicide notes offer an invaluable source of data for gaining some insight into what it was that brought the individual to adopt this form of behavior. Their importance is based upon the assumption made by this and other authors that they contain an unsolicited account of the victim's thoughts and emotions regarding his intended act and, often, what he felt was responsible for it.[6] A study of suicide in Philadelphia by Tuckman, Kleiner, and Lavell reveals that of the 742 suicides that occurred between 1951 and 1955, 24 percent left suicide notes.[7] Shneidman and Farberow note that in each year of a ten-year period between 1945 and 1954, from 12 to 15 percent of those committing suicide in Los Angeles County left suicide notes.[8]

There seems to be no significant difference in the social, mental, or physical condition of persons leaving notes and those who do not.[9] With few exceptions, suicide notes are coherent.[10]

Tuckman et al. further acknowledge: "In this study, the writers were impressed with the possibility that in a number of cases, the suicide could have resulted from a conscious 'rational' decision . . . although, to a lesser extent, unconscious factors may have been operating."[11] Having analyzed 112 notes of persons successful in suicide in the Los Angeles area, I was also taken with their rational and coherent character. The conscious rational factors were after all obvious in the notes themselves, whereas the unconscious factors to a lesser extent "may have been operating."

Most theories of suicide make some provision for both psychic and environmental factors. Whereas environmental factors are often cited and categorized by those analyzing suicide notes, none has offered an explanation of psychic factors that can be verified by the notes themselves. The psychic formulations of psychiatrists and psychologists are always of an inferred nature.

The author believes that an explanation of suicide can be empirically derived from the notes themselves without the necessity of referring to a synthetic outside system. There is no need to proceed in the traditional fashion of either imputing meaning to the notes, or, since there are essentially an infinite number of categorical distinctions to be made, categorizing them on whatever common sense grounds strike the analyst as being either potentially fruitful or expedient, e.g. demographic, environmental, physical, or psychological categories. A description of suicidal motivation and the experiences and thought processes involved in acquiring it are not likely to be arrived at without some broader theoretical perspective, which in turn is given to some empirical validation by the notes themselves. The author intends to offer such a formulation after first briefly considering some existing sociological theories of suicide.

Former Sociological Theories of Suicide

I do not wish to get involved in a critique of previous sociological theories of suicide within the limits of this paper. However, by way of giving some general indication of how this formulation differs from others, it may be noted that Durkheim,[12] Gibbs and Martin,[13] Henry and Short,[14] and Powell[15] all have in common the fact that their theories rest basically on an analysis of official suicide rates. The theories consist essentially of an explanation of these official rates by imputing meaning to the correlations that are found to exist between the rates and certain social conditions. They are not based on actual cases of suicidal persons, their beliefs, or writings.

Some of the above, while using the common base of statistical analysis of official suicide rates, incorporate psychological and psychoanalytical notions as well. Durkheim was also aware that, ultimately, if social norms were to act as a constraint, they must be internalized. Having acknowledged this, he did not involve himself in how this was to be accomplished. The author's formulation not only recognizes that norms must be internalized if they are to constrain the individual (or inversely, that the constraints of internalized norms must be overcome if one is to act contrary to them), but undertakes to set forth the process whereby this is accomplished. It also views suicide as a social fact that has its antecedents in previous social facts. It differs from Durkheim's formulation, however, in that it undertakes to establish these previous social facts through an analysis of suicide notes.

Basis of the Formulation

The data and insights upon which this formulation is based come from two main sources: 112 suicide notes of adults and adolescents who succeeded in suicide in the Los Angeles area and insights gained by the author through his two-and-one-half-year study of adolescent suicide attempters.[16]

Whereas participation in this study has provided me with many valuable insights used in the formulation, the data on which it is based are taken from the 112 suicide notes previously mentioned. The paper will offer a sampling of notes from the various categories identified by the author. These will be analyzed and discussed within the framework of a theoretical perspective, which is designed to account for the conscious deliberations that take place before the individual is able to consider and execute the act of suicide. This is seen within the broader context of what the individual must experience in order to become capable of these verbalizations. The notes provide the basis for the formulation and, at the same time, offer the reader a means of verifying it. It is the author's belief that such verification is not contingent upon these notes in particular, but that any set of notes collected from within the same cultural environment would do as well.

The key to this formulation, i.e. the concept of trust violation and how the individual accomplishes it while remaining convinced that he is a trusted person, is taken from Donald Cressey's work on embezzlement, *Other People's Money.*[17] The final form of the evolved hypothesis reads —

Trusted persons become trust violators when they conceive of themselves as having a financial problem which is nonshareable, are aware that this problem can be secretly resolved by violation of the position of financial trust, and are able to apply to their own conduct in that situation verbalizations which enable them to adjust their conceptions of themselves as users of the entrusted funds or property.[18]

This conception of trust violation is extended to the act of suicide, i.e. the individual's violation of the sacred trust of life, and to the verbalizations he must entertain in order to reconcile the image of himself as a trusted person with his act of trust violation — suicide. It followed from these considerations that an excellent source of data for this undertaking would be the transcribed accounts of these verbalizations found in suicide notes. Here the similarity with Cressey's work ends, since the method of the author in studying the above is not one of analytic induction.

Both suicides and suicide attempters are considered in this paper. The events and processes leading them to these acts are held to be equatable within the following definitions of these terms, i.e. the suicide attempt is considered as a suicide attempt only if death was intended but did not result. Persons "attempting suicide" with the intent of not dying but only of using the "attempt" as an attention-getting device, a manipulative technique, etc., were not considered by the author as suicide attempters within the limits of this paper. The intentions of persons "attempting suicide" as an attention-getting device may miscarry and result in death. Persons actually attempting suicide may, through some misinformation or fortuitous circumstance, continue to live. This in no way alters their intent or the experiences that led them to entertain the verbalizations necessary for establishing this intent. It is in this sense that suicide and suicide attempts are considered by the author to be synonymous.

These three categories of persons were distinguished from one another in the following way. The authors of the 112 notes to be discussed in this paper were all considered to be suicides based upon a designation assigned to them by the Los Angeles County Coroner's Office upon investigating the circumstances of their death. The distinction between suicide attempters and attention-getters was based upon the adolescent's account of his intentions at the time of his act. All adolescent suicide attempters in the above-mentioned study were seen within forty-eight hours of the attempt. Their intentions were related to three separate persons during their voluntary commitment at the hospital — to the attending physician who treated them in the emergency room, to the psychiatrist during a psychiatric interview, and to the author or his assistant in an interview which lasted about two hours. The designation by the author of suicide attempter was based upon a comparison and assessment of these three accounts.

Introduction to the Formulation

Nearly all of the suicide notes studied were found to fall within one of six general categories, i.e. *first form notes, sorry illness notes, not sorry illness notes, direct accusation notes, will and testament notes,* and *notes of instruction.* The sum total of all six categories of suicide notes and the explanations given for the notes taking the form they do constitute *The Formulation,* a systematic explanation for all but ten notes, i.e. 102 out of 112 notes studied by the author. The exceptions are noted later. The ten-point process to be discussed is characteristic of first form notes. Thirty-five of the 112 notes took this form. In addition, sorry illness notes also contained all or most of the characteristics found in first form notes, depending upon their length. The reader is cautioned not to view the other four forms of notes as exceptions that tend to negate the process associated with first form and sorry illness notes. These four forms and the explanations accompanying them are not exceptions but qualified additions that supplement the scope of the original ten points.

By way of analogy, consider the statement that light travels in a straight line, except when it encounters an opaque object, except in the case of refraction, except in the case of diffraction, etc. One does not say of these exceptions that they tend to negate the Principle of the Rectilinear Propagation of Light. They simply work to narrow its scope and set its limits. (The recognition and discussion of the four categories of notes cited above serve the same purpose.) To the extent that one is able to explain the exceptions in such a way that the explanations are consistent with the evidence, the sum total of these explanations constitutes a more detailed and inclusive understanding of light, or, in the case of the author's formulation, of suicide. The author also believes that the formulation will provide an explanation of suicide, within this culture, that is both empirically derived and more consistent with the evidence than any he has thus far encountered.

The Formulation

Trusted persons appear to become trust violators when they conceive of themselves as having a problem, the nature of which is a view of the past plagued by troubles, a troubled present, and the expectation of future troubles erupting unpredictably in the course of their lives. Paradoxically, these unpredictable troubles occur with absolute predictability in that it is held that they are sure to come — as sure as they are here now, unexpectedly, as sure as they arose unexpectedly in the past, and as sure as one's future existence to arise unexpectedly in the future. The problem is thus seen to be as absolute as life and must be resolved by something no less absolute than death. Since it is impossible to dispose of the problem of change (where change is viewed as unanticipated, inevitable, and inevitably for the worse), and since one sees it necessary to resolve this problem in order to live (i.e. to fulfill one's trust), and since the absolute nature of the problem makes it amenable only to absolute solutions, and since there is only one absolute solution, one finds it necessary to resolve the problem of living by dying. To put it another way, one appears to betray one's most sacred public trust by the private act of suicide.

Implicit or explicit in most of the suicide notes is the notion that "they didn't want it this way . . . but. . . ." From this perspective, they are now in a position to view themselves as blameless, i.e. trusted persons, while at the same time knowing that you will view them as trust violators because you have not experienced what they have and therefore cannot see the moral and reasonable nature of the act. With this in mind, they beg your indulgence and ask your forgiveness, for, in short, they know what they're doing, but they also know that you cannot know.

Life's problems, which one is morally obligated to resolve by way of not violating the sacred trust to live, can only be resolved by death, a not-too-pretty paradox, but from the perspective of the potential suicide, a necessary and consequently reasonable and moral view. From the absence of choice, i.e. no freedom, emerges the greatest freedom — *the recognition of necessity* — stemming from the apparent lack of choice. Thus it is that the suicidal person sees in the act of suicide at long last the potential for the freedom he has sought in life. This can be seen in the notes themselves. The note writers are rarely depressed or hostile. The notes are by and large very even, as though at the time of writing the suffering no longer existed and a resolution to the problem had been reached. Tuckman states that 51 percent of the notes he studied expressed *positive affect without hostility* and another 25 percent expressed *neutral affect.*[19] This is further supported by the finding of Farberow et al. that the period of highest risk was not during the depression or "illness" but just after it when the patient seemed much improved.[20]

First Form Notes

The outline presented below describes the formal aspects of a process that the individual must first experience in order to be able to seriously entertain suicide and then actually attempt it. The extent to which this process is operative will be illustrated through an analysis of first form notes. The extent to which the other five forms of notes deviate from the characteristics found in first form notes will be discussed in the explanations accompanying each of the five remaining forms. The sum total of all six forms of notes and their accompanying explanations constitute *The Formulation,* i.e. a systematic rational explanation of suicide based upon the suicide's own accounts at the time of the act.

Durkheim went to great lengths to show that private acts contrary to the public trust are irrational and/or immoral and constrained by public sanctions from ever occurring. In order to overcome these constraints and appear to others as a trust violator, the private individual must (1) be faced with an unexpected, intolerable, and unsolvable problem; (2) view this not as an isolated unpleasant incident, but within the context of a long biography of such troubled situations and the expectation of future ones; (3) believe that death is the only absolute answer to this apparent absolute dilemma of life; (4) come to this point of view (a) by way of an increasing social isolation whereby he is unable to share his problem with the person or persons who must share it if it is to be resolved or (b) being isolated from the cure of some incurable illness which in turn isolates him from health and the community, thereby doubly ensuring the insolubility of the problem; (5) overcome the social constraints, i.e. the social norms he had internalized whereby he views suicide as irrational and/or immoral; (6) succeed in this because he feels himself less an integral part of the society than the others and therefore is held less firmly by its bonds; (7) succeed in accomplishing Step 6 by applying to his intended suicide a verbalization that enables him to adjust his conception of himself as a trusted person with his conception of himself as a trust violator; (8) succeed in doing this by defining the situation such that the problem is (a) not of his own making, (b) unresolved, but not from any lack of personal effort, and (c) not given to any resolution known to him except death (he doesn't want it this way, but . . . it's "the only way out"); (9) in short, define death as necessary by the above process and in so doing remove all choice and with it sin and immorality; and finally, (10) make some provision for ensuring against the recurrence of these problems in the afterlife.

Thirty-five out of 112 notes were first form notes and expressed all or most of the above aspects, depending on their length. All first form notes are characterized by the author's begging of forgiveness or request for indulgence. The following will serve to illustrate the general tenor:

It is hard to say why you don't want to live. I have only one real reason. The three people I have in the world which I love don't want me.

Tom, I love you so dearly but you have told me you don't want me and don't love me. I never thought you would let me go this far, but I am now at the end which is the best thing for you. You have so many problems and I am sorry I added to them.

Daddy, I hurt you so much and I guess I really hurt myself. You only wanted the very best for me and you must believe this is it.

Mommy, you tried so hard to make me happy and to make things right for all of us. I love you too so very much. You did not fail, I did.

I had no place to go so I am back where I always seem to find peace. I have failed in everything I have done and I hope I do not fail in this.

I love you all dearly and am sorry this is the way I have to say goodbye.

Please forgive me and be happy.

Your wife and daughter

First, the problem is not of their own making. At first glance the suicide seems to be saying just the opposite. "You did not fail, I did," "I have failed in everything." However, having acknowledged this, she states: "Tom, I love you so dearly but you have told me you don't want me and don't love me. *I never thought you would let me go this far.*" Then, of course, she loves them. It is they who do not love her, and this is the problem.

Second, a long-standing history of problems. "Mommy, you tried so hard to make me happy and to make things right for all of us. I love you too so very much. You did not fail, I did," or "Tom . . . you have so many problems and I am sorry I added to them," etc. It seems from this that she has created a long-standing history of problems. She was, nevertheless, subject to them as well. "Daddy, I hurt you so much and I guess I *really hurt myself.*"

Third, the escalation of problems of late beyond human endurance. "It is hard to say why you don't want to live. I have only one real reason. The three people I have in the world which I love don't want me," or "Tom, I love you so dearly but you have told me you don't want me and don't love me."

These particular problems are clearly of recent origin and of greater magnitude than any she had previously experienced. By her own account, had she experienced problems of this order before, she would have taken her life before, since they led to her losing what had previously constituted sufficient reason for her to go on living.

Fourth, death must be seen as necessary. "It is hard to say why you don't want to live. I have only one real reason. The three people I have in the world which I love don't want me," or ". . . but now I'm at the end . . . ," and finally, "I love you all dearly and am sorry this is the way *I have to* say goodbye."

Fifth, beg your indulgence. "I love you all dearly and am *sorry* this is the way I have to say goodbye."

Sixth, they know what they're doing but know you cannot know. "Daddy . . . You only wanted the very best for me and *you must believe this is it.*"

It is the author's opinion that the suicide's message in point (3) is the same as that given by nearly all the others who attempt or succeed in suicide, insofar as this is a particular case of the general condition of *a progressive social isolation from meaningful relationships.*

Ellen West, whose case history is perhaps the most famous, wrote the following in her diary less than a year before taking her life:

. . .by this fearful illness I am withdrawing more and more from people. I feel myself excluded from all real life. I am quite isolated. I sit in a glass ball. I see people through a glass wall, their voices come to me muffled. I have an unutterable longing to get to them. I scream, but they do not hear me. I stretch out my arms toward them; but my hands merely beat against the walls of my glass ball.[21]

All of the remaining first form notes have all or most of the above characteristics in common. *All of the notes in this class, without exception, beg forgiveness or indulgence on the part of the survivors.*

Illness Notes

Requests for forgiveness or indulgence may be omitted when the writer feels that the public may have made exceptions to its general indignation at suicide, exceptions that should be known to all, e.g. in the case of persons suffering from an incurable disease, suffering great pain, etc. In such cases, the suicide may feel that no apologies are necessary, and requests for forgiveness may be included or excluded, due to the ambiguity surrounding the degree of public acceptance of the above view.

Thirty-four notes were included in the illness category. Twenty-two of these omitted requests for forgiveness; twelve included them. This category of notes has most of the same general characteristics as those of the first form. How many conditions of the first form notes are met by those of the illness category depends primarily on their length. The two formal distinguishing features of these two sets of notes are that the illness set may or may not beg forgiveness for the reasons stated above, and, secondly, the source of the problem is generally better defined and restricted to the area of illness, pain, etc., and its social and personal implications to the individual. Some examples of illness notes follow.

Sorry Illness Notes:

Dearly Beloved Children: For the last three weeks I have lost my blood circulation in my feet and in my hands. I can hardly hold a spoon in my hand. Before I get a stroke on top of my other troubles of my legs I decided that this would be the easier for me. I have always loved you all dearly. Think of me kindly sometimes. Please forgive me. I cannot endure any more pains.

Lovingly, mother

Not Sorry Illness Notes:

If you receive this letter you will know that I have emptied my bottle of sleeping pills.

And a second note by the same author addressed to the same person included the line: "Surely there must be a justifiable mercy death."

Another reads —

Dear Jane: You are ruining your health and your life just for me, and I cannot let you do it. The pains in my face seem worse every day and there is a limit to what a man can take. I love you dear.

Bill

Notes of Direct Accusation

None of the notes in this class beg forgiveness or offer an apology. The suicide feels that not only is the problem not of his making, but he knows who is responsible for having to commit suicide. As a result, he feels righteously indignant and omits requests for indulgence, especially when the note is directed to the guilty party. Direct accusation notes are generally very brief — rarely more than a few lines long. Ten of the 112 notes studied were of the direct accusation type. For example:

You Bob and Jane caused this — this all.

Goodbye, Jane. I couldn't take no more from you. Bob

Mary, I hope you're satisfied. Bill

If you had read page 150 of *Red Ribbons* this wouldn't have happened.

Last Will and Testaments and Notes of Instructions

None of these notes contained requests for forgiveness or indulgence either. This omission, as in the above case, results from the form of the notes themselves. These notes usually concern themselves exclusively with the manner in which the suicide's property is to be apportioned. They give no mention of the circumstances of the suicide and, as a result, there is no need for the notewriter to admit guilt or request forgiveness. None of them do so.

Last Will and Testaments:

I hereby bequeath all my worldly goods and holdings to Bill Smith. $1 to Chris Baker, $1 to Ann Barnes. Signed in sober consideration.

Mary Smith

Notes of Instructions

The following are some examples of notes of instructions. They are almost always very brief and the above comments regarding last will and testaments apply here as well.

Call Jane. S Street, Apt. 2. Thank Officer No. 10.

I have gone down to the ocean. Pick out the cheapest coffin Jones Bros. has. I don't remember the cost. I'll put my purse in the trunk of the car.

Precautions Taken to Exclude This World's Problems from the Next World

To guard against the eventuality of a similar set of troubles erupting in the afterlife, the very thing one is dying to overcome, one of six possible courses of action are formulated and internalized. These forms first came to the attention of the author while studying suicidal adolescents and suicide notes and will be the topic of the next chapter, where we will consider the role of religion in suicide.

It is true, of course, that Durkheim also dealt with the role of religion in suicide by establishing the degree of social integration within various religions as the constraining factor against suicide, rather than the religious dogma per se. However, what has not been discussed is the way in which religious dogma, specifically intended to prevent suicide, can with the proper rationalization serve to encourage suicide. The following discussion deals with why and how this is actually accomplished by the potential suicide.

Finally, the author acknowledges that some exceptions occurred within the above categories. However, among the 112 suicide notes studied, the paucity of cases falling into a residual category is heartening. There were ten of these in all, four of which contained the only elements of humor found in all of the notes. For example:

Please do not disturb. Someone sleeping
(Hung on the dashboard of his car).

Conclusions

If it is true as Hume believed that ". . . such is our natural horror of death, that small motives will never be able to reconcile us to it . . ."[22] it is also true that the horror of life is no small motive. I believe that most people prefer the uncertainties of life to the uncertainties of death, because in life they have defined for themselves the possibility of certain sets of events occurring and live in the expectation that anything can happen, i.e. life is full of ups and downs. If one's view of life excludes uncertainty, i.e. life is not full of ups and downs — only downs, and anything can't happen — things can only get worse, then one might better try the uncertainties of death for its very ambiguity allows for either. By accepting death one provides the possibility of resolving life's problems, while at the same time ensuring against future problems (or at least providing the possibility of resolving future problems when they arise).

I believe it is necessary to take seriously what the suicide writes in attempting to explain to the survivors, as a reasonable person, why he is committing suicide and suggest that the reader will be aided in this task by applying the formulation presented by the author. I am further convinced that a fuller understanding of suicide will emerge only if one's procedures for transcending the data do not end by ignoring it and that the data transcended ought to have some direct relation to the real life phenomenon under study, i.e. suicide.

Having considered the virtues of a phenomenological approach to suicide and how it reveals both the nature and necessity of moral justifications, we will go on to Chapter 4, where we consider in greater detail the role of moral justifications within the context of religion.

REFERENCES

1. Emile Durkheim, *Suicide: A Study in Sociology.* New York, The Free Press, 1951, pp. 297-298.
2. A youth who was prematurely tired, in Ruth Cavan, *Suicide.* Chicago, University of Chicago Press, 1928, p. 242.
3. Edwin S. Shneidman and Norman L. Farberow, Appendix: Genuine and simulated suicide notes, in *Clues to Suicide.* New York, McGraw-Hill, 1957, p. 197.
4. Charles William Wahl, Suicide as a magical act, in Edwin S. Shneidman and Norman L. Farberow (Eds.), *Clues to Suicide.* New York, McGraw-Hill, 1957, p. 23.
5. C. Wright Mills, Situated actions and vocabularies of motive. *American Sociological Review*, 5:909, December, 1940.
6. Jacob Tuckman, Robert J. Kleiner, and Martha Lavell, Emotional content of suicide notes. *American Journal of Psychiatry*, July, 1959, p. 59.
7. Ibid.
8. Shneidman and Farberow, op. cit., p. 198.
9. Tuckman et al., op. cit, p. 59, and Shneidman and Farberow, op. cit., p. 48.

10. Tuckman et al., op. cit., p. 60.
11. Ibid., p. 62.
12. Emile Durkheim, op. cit.
13. Jack P. Gibbs and Walter T. Martin, *Status Integration and Suicide.* Eugene, Oregon, University of Oregon Press, 1964.
14. Andrew F. Henry and James F. Short, *Suicide and Homicide.* Glencoe, Illinois, The Free Press, 1954.
15. Elwin H. Powell, "Occupational status and suicide: Toward a redefinition of anomie." *American Sociological Review, 23*:131, April, 1950.
16. Adolescent Attempted Suicide Study, supported by the National Institute of Mental Health and conducted at the Los Angeles County General Hospital under the direction of Joseph D. Teicher, M.D., Professor of Psychiatry, University of Southern California School of Medicine, and Jerry Jacobs, Ph.D., Research Associate, University of Southern California School of Medicine.
17. Donald R. Cressey, *Other People's Money.* Glencoe, Illinois, The Free Press, 1951.
18. Ibid., p. 30.
19. Tuckman et al., op. cit., p. 61.
20. Norman L. Farberow, Edwin S. Shneidman, and Robert E. Litman, The suicidal patient and the physician. *Mind, 1*:69, March, 1963.
21. Ludwig Brinswanger, The case of Ellen West, in Rollo May et al. (Eds.), *Existence.* New York, Basic Books, 1958, p. 256.
22. David Hume, Of suicide, in Alasdair MacIntyre (Ed.), *Hume's Ethical Writings.* New York, Collier Books, 1965, p. 305.

Chapter 4

THE USE OF RELIGION
IN CONSTRUCTING THE MORAL
JUSTIFICATION OF SUICIDE

T HE analysis found in Chapter 3 dealt primarily with how the
suicide was able to overcome the moral constraints implicit
and explicit in social norms. Overcoming the constraints of social
norms is only one important moral issue with which the individual
contemplating suicide must contend.

Another moral issue faced by the suicide is more directly
associated with religion per se. The topic of religion and suicide
has generally been dealt with from one of three broad perspectives: how religion works to prevent suicide by specifically pro-
hibiting it, how religion effects social suicide rates as a result of
the relative extent of social integration between members of any
particular religious sect, and how religion may work to encourage
suicide by sanctioning it in certain circumstances.

Examples of the condemnation of suicide by various religious
sects are numerous. The Koran is explicit in its prohibition of suicide. "The question is asked: 'What ought one to think of suicide?" And the answer is: "It is a much greater crime than homicide." At yet another point, the faithful are enjoined: "Neither
slay yourselves, for God is merciful toward you, and whoever doth
this maliciously and wickedly, He will surely cast him to be
broiled in the hellfire."[1]

Although there is no specific prohibition of suicide in the Old
or New Testaments, Catholics, Protestants, and Jews are clear in
their prohibition of it. The idea (discounted by Durkheim) that
the perspective of religious teachings toward life, death, and the
hereafter have little or nothing to do with suicide rates of Catholics,
Protestants, and Jews is not adhered to by all. For example, in
a discussion of suicide in Jewish history, Dublin notes the following:

> This interesting phenomenon (the low rates of suicide among Jews) can
> be explained by the attitude of the religious Jew toward life and in the
> philosophic outlook of Judaism. Suicide is unthinkable — and it is un-
> thinkable because throughout the Old Testament runs the theme of
> the sacredness of life. . . . Their usual attitude is expressed by Job who,
> when his wife wished him to give up the struggle against adverse fortune
> and bade him "curse God and die," answered in the true spirit of sub-
> mission: "Thou speakest as one of the foolish women speaketh.
> What! Shall we receive good at the hand of God and shall we not re-
> ceive evil?" And naturally the temperament whose faith is strong
> enough, when beset with trials and tribulations, to maintain that "the
> Lord gave, and the Lord hath taken away; blessed be the name of the
> Lord," is not one inclined toward suicide.[2]

Catholicism is even more explicit in its prohibition of suicide.
In this case, the act is considered a mortal sin and, as with
Mohammedism, a graver crime than homicide. "The church. . .
eventually adopted the extreme view, holding Judas Iscariot's
betrayal of Christ as a lesser sin than his suicide. From permission to kill in defense of one's life, the inference was drawn that
suicide is indeed more reprehensible than homicide."[3]

So explicit is the prohibition of Catholicism and Protestantism
against suicide that Durkheim believed that the restraints against
it were equally binding for the adherents of both and, therefore,
could not per se explain the differences found in the suicide
rates.

> . .Both prohibit suicide with equal emphasis; not only do they penalize
> it morally with great severity, but both teach that a new life begins
> beyond the tomb where men are punished for their evil actions, and
> Protestantism just as well as Catholicism numbers suicide among
> them. Finally, in both cults these prohibitions are of divine origin; they
> are represented not as logical conclusions of correct reason, but God

Himself is their authority. Therefore, if Protestantism is less unfavorable to the development of suicide, it is not because of a different attitude from that of Catholicism. Thus, if both religions have the same precepts with respect to this particular matter, their dissimilar influence on suicide must proceed from one of the more general characteristics differentiating them.[4]

If the above is a convenient assumption to make in the furtherance, indeed maintenance of the argument that the relative degree of social integration within these religions is the general characteristic differentiating them, it is nevertheless a questionable one. There is good reason to suppose that the religious constraints on Catholics and Protestants with respect to suicide are in fact differentially binding and might effect the higher rate of suicide among the latter. Douglas has dealt with this aspect from one perspective.[5] The author will deal with it from yet another later in this paper.

This leads us to the third and last broad perspective on religion and suicide noted earlier, i.e., the way in which religion may work to encourage suicide by sanctioning it in specific instances. Perhaps the most frequent reference to this last perspective is *suttee*, the Hindu widow's act of self-immolation on the funeral pyre of her husband. Through this act she becomes. . ."the goddess Sati herself, reincarnate; the sakti, or projected life-energy of her spouse." For the widow to go on living, according to this doctrine, ensures that she survives in the realization that she is "unreal, nonexistent, false, untrue, improper;. . .bad, wicked, evil, vile."[6]

Apart from this and other obvious forms of religiously sanctioned suicide, such as the Japanese hara-kiri, are the less obvious historical exceptions to Christianity's abhorrence of suicide. "Exaltation of 'suicide' in early Christian philosophy may be found in the calculated improvidence of martyrs and the enthusiasm for death on the part of ascetics, as well as in the glorification of suicide committed in the defense of virtue."[7]

An earlier example is found in the ambiguities of Roman law. While certain suicides were punishable, as in the case of a master or the state's claim upon the life of a slave or soldier, other suicides were exempt. Some examples of exemptions were suicides caused by "impatience of pain or sickness, some grief or by another cause."[8] In short, the range of acceptable suicides for persons other than those considered property was great. Some indication of this acceptability is given by Cicaro: "God Himself has given a valid reason as He did. . .to Socrates and. .Cato, and often to many others, then of a surety your true wise man will joyfully pass forthwith from the darkness here into the light beyond."[9]

Even the Jews seem to have allowed for certain exceptions to the sacredness of life. Four instances of suicide are found in the Old Testament: Samson, Ibimelech, Ahithophel, and Saul.[10] Whereas, Saul ordered himself slain by his armor-bearer, the first three were cases of persons taking their own lives.

It should be noted in concluding this discussion that notwithstanding the exceptions (some of which are noted above), Catholicism, Protestantism, and Judaism have all taken (to one extent or another) a common stand in attempting to discourage suicide. In spite of the universality of the prohibition taken by the major religions toward suicide, not everyone shared in this moral indignation. Perhaps the most eloquent argument in the defense of suicide came from Hume, who, having noted the absence of prohibitions against it in either the Old or New Testaments, holds that in order to be a crime, the act of suicide must be a transgression against God, society, or the self. Having argued well that it was none of these, he concludes, "If suicide be supposed a crime, tis only cowardice can impel us to it. If it be no crime, both prudence and courage should engage us to rid ourselves at once of existence, when it becomes a burden. Tis the only way that we can then be useful to society, by setting an example which, if imitated, would preserve to every one his chance for happiness in life and would effectually free him from all danger or misery.[11]

To the extent that the Pope and not Hume held sway over the minds of Christendom, the former view was by far the favored one, except, unfortunately, in the minds of the suicides themselves. For although few are capable of marshalling so eloquent a defense of suicide as Hume, many others have of necessity tried. The suicide's need to resolve, to his own satisfaction, the moral prohibitions against suicide is the central concern of this paper.

The critical question is whether or not the individual who has in desperation reached the point of entertaining suicide as a possible resolution to his problems is able to resolve to his own satisfaction the binding effects of the social and religious moral prohibitions against it. An interesting sociological problem is how he succeeds in doing so.

The following process, based upon the author's previous works, describes the ordering of events by which the individual is led to become suicidal:

1. A longstanding history of problems.
2. A more recent escalation of problems, i.e. the inability to resolve old problems at the same time that many new ones have been added.
3. The progressive failure of available adaptive techniques for coping with old and increasing problems, which leads the individual to feel a progressive isolation from meaningful social relationships.
4. The final stage — the days and weeks immediately preceding the suicide — at which time the individual feels he has experienced an abrupt and unanticipated dissolution of any remaining meaningful relationships and the prospects of ever establishing them in the future. He experiences, in short, "the end of hope."[12]

In brief, the potential suicide feels the necessity of taking his own life because from his perspective, he has attempted (to no avail) every other possible alternative available to him for dealing with his problems. Death is seen as the only answer. . .the only possible resolution to the unbearable and insoluble problems of life.

Having been subject to this sequence of events and come to the above conclusion, one is now able to entertain the ten-point process described in the author's previous work (*see* Footnote 5) by which the potential suicide resolves the social prohibitions against suicide. Having succeeded in this, it remains only for him to resolve the moral restraints implicit or explicit in religious prohibitions. This leads to a fourth important and badly neglected perspective from which to view suicide and religion, i.e. *the way in which religious dogma, intended specifically to discourage suicide, is interpreted by the suicidal person in such a way as to encourage it.* The processes noted above deal with the way in which the suicide convinces himself that he is blameless and without sin (the contradictory edicts of religious dogma notwithstanding), by convincing himself that he has no choice. The act in the final analysis is seen as a case of necessity. Since sin (mortal or otherwise) presupposes that the individual has a choice and elects, for whatever reason, to do wrong, he is blameless, inasmuch as he has not chosen to kill himself, *but feels rather that ,he must.* Since freedom is *the recognition of necessity,* the potential suicide feels just prior to the act that he is finally free. An account of the final entry in the diary of Ellen West notes that —

> On the third day of being home she is transformed. At breakfast she eats butter and sugar, at noon she eats so much that — for the first time in thirteen years! — she is satisfied by her food and gets really full. She takes a walk with her husband. . .is in a positively festive mood, and all heaviness seems to have fallen away from her. . . . In the evening she takes a lethal dose of poison and on the following morning she is dead. "She looked as she had never looked in life — calm, happy and peaceful."[13]

An excerpt from a long suicide note written by a physician, relating his thoughts and setting his affairs in order, reads —

Although I am upset now, it is surprising how calm I feel about ending it.

Toward the end of the same four-page typewritten note it says —

I am quite determined and less afraid. 2500 MGM of seconal and some_____(illegible) ahead of this should do the trick.[14]

Part of another suicide note reads —

Oh Bob I love you, you too Betty, Mary, Ralph and Jim. Just remember that mother wanted the best for all of you, to play with you, go places with you. I miss all the good times. *I can't stay locked in this room forever. I want to be free.*[15]

The anticipation of a final relief is a general condition to the suicide taking place. An excerpt from a rather lengthy suicide note reads —

...There must be a reward for this miserable experience called life. Life would be utterly pointless without it. . . .*Be consoled (my wife) by the happy thought that leaving this world is a release from sorrow. . . .*[16]

Another note, a case of murder-suicide reads —

To the police station: I have now been unemployed for four years and we are starting to lack even the necessities. *We have decided to go with our children into the hereafter where no unemployment exists and where one is not surrounded by creatures and human beasts.* We ask that you don't get mad at us for doing this, because we have no other solution. . . .[17]

Part of another note reads —

Somewhere in this pile is your answers. I couldn't find it. Mom, you should have known what was about to happen after I told you my troubles. *Now I will get my rest. . . .*[18]

An excerpt from the diary of a suicide reads —

What's the use? *Death only holds forth relief.* I cannot look back on a really happy day. Lighthearted and merry have I been on occasion, but seldom a day without morbid thoughts sometime or another. . . .[19]

However, prior to actually attempting to take his own life, the individual may beg God to spare him the necessity of resorting to suicide. After all, only God has the right: "The Lord giveth and the Lord taketh away."

I want to move to Canada. God, I know I can't live here anymore. No, not in this horrible city. It is wicked, it is cruel. I can't escape it. No, not even in my dreams. What is a dream? Which is the nightmare? Sleep promises escape from this misery —only sleep too is deceitful. Who will end it all for me? I try, but I cannot. I don't even have strength to end this pain. This ceaseless, unrelenting pain. Why was I ever born? What a cruel trick my mother played on me. Is there no limit? I will seek my relief in the grave. God, why? Why do you do this to me? Are you God or are you the Devil? God must be a Devil! Yes it is the Devil I have been speaking to. *If there is a God, please let him hear me and end my agony.* Who is my father? Is he the Devil? No, I am the Devil and there is no death, there is no end. *God please release me in death.* [20]

As we will see in the next chapter, the request to have one's life taken is sometimes addressed to a husband or other loved one, instead of to God. They are, after all, next in line for the *right* or *duty* to do so. This would be especially true in the case of the non-believer. It is no accident that most murders and nearly all cases of murder-suicide are family affairs.[21]

In the above case, the expectation is that one's problems will be resolved in death. Having considered the way in which death is viewed as the only respite to life's problems leads us to the specific way in which religious dogma may work to encourage suicide. There would be little point in resolving one's problems in this life, only to incur a new set as bad or worse in the here-after. The suicide's ability to convince himself that death will reduce or eliminate his problems is the final ingredient for the pre-viously described peace and calm found among suicides imme-diately preceding their act. It is in his search for a means of achieving this outlook that religion holds a promise. The suicide is able to acquire this optimistic outlook toward the hereafter by adopting one of several situated interpretations toward existing religious dogma. I will list these forms of interpretation and give illustrations of each from the suicide's or suicide at-tempter's own accounts as taken either from suicide notes and diaries or detailed case histories.

First, the suicidal person who had previously been a diligent churchgoer and considered himself religious may abruptly cease attending church and, at the same time, start considering himself a nonbeliever. In doing so, he disposes of the prospect of Heaven and Hell and simultaneously secures for himself all the benefits of the atheist with respect to any future problems. It is one way to resolve the ambiguities implicit in the Heaven and Hell scheme and ensure that suicide is in fact the ultimate solution to life's problems. From this perspective, one is able to view suicide as a way to end it all. By excluding the possibility of a future existence, one excludes the possibility of future problems as well. The case histories of fifty adolescent suicide attempters, studied by the author, offer several examples of this form of resolution. Excerpts from the case history of a seventeen-year-old girl who attempted suicide by ingesting about 40 Sominex® tablets provides an interesting case in point. The case record reads —

> Mother feels that Mr. M. didn't take Joan's suicide attempt very seriously — "he's very cool about most things." Mother states that she was very upset, but not really shocked since Joan had discussed suicide many times in the past. Mrs. M. believes the prospect of going to Hell had frightened Joan out of it before.

> She (Joan) does not consider herself to be a religious person, although some of her friends are religious. She used to be very religious, but no more. "It wasn't doing me any good. . . People always talk about hearing God speak to them, but I never heard God talk to me."

Joan seemed to have begun losing interest in religion within several months of the attempt.

As another example from these case histories a fourteen-year-old Caucasian male suicide attempter notes, "Tom participates in activities sponsored by the Congregation Church where he used to attend regularly. Tom claims to be an atheist 'right now.' He thinks that when a person dies, he's just dead."[22]

A second solution to the problem of the hereafter is illustrated by the suicidal person who suddenly "gets religion." These cases were more numerous among fifty adolescent suicide attempters noted above than were those who abruptly abandoned religion. Among these were those who may have previously attended church to one extent or another, but did not count themselves among the faithful. Many felt in retrospect that they were hypocrites. They generally felt a distressing ambiguity about whether or not they would go to Heaven. It is not uncommon for such persons to suddenly make such inquiries as: "Does God forgive anything?", or "Will God forgive suicide?". It is generally the case that those to whom the question is put, believing that He does, or anxious for the convert, or for whatever other reason, will answer, "Yes, if you really believe." At this point, the person does all that is within his grasp to get religion, and really believe.

The following are some examples taken from the case records:

A suicide note left by a sixteen-year-old Caucasian girl who attempted suicide by ingesting twenty-five to thirty Dilantin® capsules reads —

Please forgive me, God I am so mixed up or else I don't know what I really want of life. I love Mom, Joan, Lucy, and everyone else in the world so much. I thought and almost fully convinced myself that I was not fully wanted or accepted in the world. . . . In my heart I know there is a Christ everywhere in the world that is being with everyone, every second of every day, and He represents God in every way. I know that in my brain (mind) I think evil things about different situations and sometimes I think that Christ never existed. But my heart is always strong and that when I think that Christ never lived I know that in my heart He did. I love God and Jesus Christ and the world so much that it really breaks my heart to see that I am trying to kill myself. . . . No matter what I said to Mom and Joan and everyone else, I love Mom more than myself, I think I didn't mean the things I said in anger or otherwise to people. I am sorry for all the things I ever said that were sarcastic or mean. *Mother thinks that there is no Hell or Heaven and I know there is a Hell and Heaven. I don't want to go to the devil, God, so please forgive me to what I have just done. Frank Jones says that if I believe in and accept Jesus that I would go to heaven. Some people say that if you ask forgiveness to God for things you do to yourself or others, that He would forgive you (if you believe in Jesus and love him). . . . If I were to live I might never have been at peace with myself. . . . Heaven is so peaceful and the earth is very troublesome and terrifying.* [23]

In this case, as in the one to follow, both the adolescent and her mother reported that the girl's serious preoccupation with religion began abruptly within the last year.

The following statement is taken from the verbatim accounts of a transcribed therapy session with a sixteen-year-old Caucasian girl who attempted suicide by ingesting thirty-one Miltown® tablets:

Doctor: Have you had any religious experiences?

Teenager: Billy Graham Crusade in 1963 (This was a year before the attempt).

Doctor: Umhm.

Teenager: That's when I really accepted Jesus.

Doctor: Did you have an experience?

Teenager: I started to cry. I started to realize that I'd been a hypocrite for all those years, saying I was a Christian, but I'd been beating up on kids and stuff like that. That isn't a Christian.

Doctor: Umhm.

Teenager: And lying — that isn't Christian. And stealing.[24]

The account goes on to describe the ways in which she has since tried to become a "good Christian."

A third position is that of the atheists whose past outlook, being consistent with their present needs, requires no revisions. However, even the atheists may have a second thought and take some added precaution just in case. An example of this is a seventeen-year-old Mexican-American male who attempted suicide by ingesting twenty-five "reds" (Benzedrine® capsules). The case history notes, "Jimmy does not consider himself to be religious, nor are any of his friends. He doesn't know if suicide is a sin or not, but in either case, he believes that sin is forgiven and that there is no life after death. Jimmy doesn't attend the Catholic Church or any other, but said he was planning to go to confession next Saturday".[25]

Another adolescent, an eighteen-year-old Negro male who attempted suicide by drinking battery acid, related the following to the interviewer:

> Between the ages of 15 and 16, James attended the Four Square Church very regularly with his father to please him. After he left his father, his church attendance ended. James does not consider himself religious. He does not believe in an afterlife; "If you're dead you're dead." However, during the interview, whenever he hesitated about answering certain personal questions, he told the interviewer that he would "tell that to a priest." In fact, he thought someone should let a priest know that he was in trouble so that he could come to the hospital and James could confess his sins to him.[26]

A fourth position that may be taken is that of the religious person who, although he is aware that suicide is a mortal sin and that he is going to Hell for it, tries to kill himself anyway. This seems to be contradictory to the position previously outlined by the author, in that it is generally held that one's personal situation is unlikely to improve in Hell. However, a closer analysis reveals that the suicide's position in such cases is equivocal. He is not certain that he is going to Hell or, if he is, he is not certain that things are worse there. The very ambiguity of death allows at least for the possibility that things will be better. Such a view is not a difficult one to risk, if one is already convinced that things couldn't be worse than they are at present. The following example of this line of reasoning is taken from the diary of a suicide:

I am sad and lonely. Oh, God how lonely. I am starving. Oh, God, I am ready for the last, last chance. I have taken two already, they were not right. Life was the first chance, marriage the second, and *now I am ready for death, the last chance. It cannot be worse than it is here.* [27]

Another note, this one from a case of murder-suicide, reads —

Dearest darling Jane: (his separated wife): Don't hate me for taking the life of our son. I have tried in so many ways to send him off with someone, but he would just cry when I speak of it. He said I want you. He wants me. *I'm going to Hell and he wants me.* What do you do with a loving son like that? Let him suffer or take him with you?.... Why did God give me this brain? Why doesn't He stop me? He puts us on earth and we do what is best, good and bad. I just wanted one more chance.... If I only had one more chance. *Will God give me one more chance?* [28]

Having noted that his wife would not give him another chance and that the friend with whom his wife ran off would not give him another chance (he called the friend to tell him he was about to kill himself, to which the friend replied: "...I'm sorry you have to do it this way."), he asks, "Will God give me another chance?" At the opening of the note his going to Hell seems a certainty. However, by its closing there is at least a possibility that God will give him another chance.

Still another note reads —

They say you go to Hell for taking your life. . .there was only one thing I wanted and I drove her so far away that there is no sense kidding myself anymore. . . . *Maybe where I'm going it won't be so lonely.*[29]

A further example from the case histories of adolescent suicide attempters is the account of a sixteen-year-old Caucasian male, who attempted suicide by ingesting forty aspirins:

I knew I'd go to Hell, but I didn't care what people thought. I probably did hurt my parents, but I didn't do it to make them feel bad. . . .

The record continues —

He is "half and half" religious person. He is Catholic and used to attend Catholic Church every week. He had a spotty attendance ever since the family moved to L.A. about a year ago. He believes that suicide is a sin, but "sometimes you don't care." He believes in Heaven and Hell, but "sometimes I'm doubtful."[30]

Another short suicide note, one of the few the author has encountered with an element of humor, reads —

Goodbye kid, you couldn't help it. Tell that brother of yours, when he gets where I'm going I hope I'm a foreman down there. I might be able to do something for him.[31]

The humorous element aside, it is clear that if he does become foreman, he might be able to do something for himself as well. In any event, he hopes so.

A subset of the perspective noted above, i.e. the possibility (if not certainty) of a better life in the next world, is to be found in those notes requesting that the survivors pray for them or that God forgive them. Here, as in the form noted above, the very ambiguity of death allows for a renewed hope for a better life in the hereafter. The following are some examples of this:

I know I am mentally ill. . .and know this is the only way out. *I ask forgiveness of God* and my beloved family. I love them all, but life is not worth living the way I am. I just can't go on the way I am. . . . I have killed myself. *God help me.*[32]

Dear Mary: I'm just too tired and sick of trying to continue. Sorry it had to be this way. I'm sure everything will work out for the best. Keep everything as quiet as possible. Say I had a heart attack. As ever, Bill. *God forgive me.* And God bless you and John.[33]

Dear Brothers and Sisters: I am so sorry to do this thing, but I am very sick and unhappy and cannot continue on. *Please do not feel sorry for me because I am sure I will be better off. . . . Pray for my soul and God bless you all.* Bob.[34]

Nobody needs to put flowers on my grave. They did nothing for me while I was alive. *My dear Hedeli forgive your father. He had no choice. May God forgive me.*[35]

Everything was tried to save me. Forgive me, and don't feel badly. Grant me rest. *Pray God be merciful to me.* The lake shall be my grave. Your tired M. . . .[36]

Still another kind of salvation in the hereafter that the potential suicide may entertain centers around the idea of a happy reunion. This may take one of three forms: their returning in an old or new form to rejoin those on earth; their remaining in heaven and the others joining them; or their joining those already deceased. The following is an example of reincarnation, the first form of reunion:

Dear Sister, don't be afraid for my sake. *I will soon come back or you will soon hear from me.* Love, Idy.[37]

The notion of the dead communicating with the living is not so novel as one might suppose. For example, Bishop Pike claimed that his son (a suicide at the age of twenty-two) gave him the following message after his death:

I am sorry I did this. I had problems. I wanted out. I wish I had carried on and worked on the problems in more familiar surroundings.[38]

The Bishop, addressing an overflow audience at a Berkeley church, went on to say: ". . .If Christ talked to his disciples after his death, then why can't we all do the same?"[39]

The adolescent suicide attempters also provide examples of this reincarnation interpretation of religious dogma. Mary H. is a sixteen-year-old Negro girl. Her case history states, "Mary does not consider herself to be a religious person, but she does attend the Methodist Church. . .One of the most important aspects of her religion is that she believes in reincarnation. . . ."[40]

It need hardly be pointed out that reincarnation is not an important aspect of Methodist teaching. However, such religious contradictions were not uncommon among the adolescent suicide attempters. For example, parents had in several instances pointed out to the adolescent after the attempt that suicide was a mortal sin. At this point the adolescent began to feel very guilty and to act as though he had never heard of this before (even though suicide was specifically prohibited).

Another example from the case histories of the use of reincarnation is that of a fifteen-year-old Jewish boy, who until moving to Los Angeles about a year ago, attended an Orthodox synagogue regularly. His mother also claims that until that time she had kept a kosher home. The case history notes, ". . .Milton claims that he is not religious at all and that most of his friends aren't either. He does, it seems, believe in reincarnation. Having mentioned this, he refused to discuss it any further. . . ."[41]

The following are two examples of the second form of reunion:

Dear Edna and Fritz: I thank you both for your kindness, patience, and care. I can no longer stand my nervousness. I am sorry to make you who have been so good to me suffer. All the people with whom I've been in contact were not very nice to me. Please forgive me everything I've done to you. . . . *May God forgive me*, I can't stand it any longer. *We will meet in the afterlife.* . . .[42]

My dearest darling Rose: *By the time you read this I will have crossed the divide to wait for you. Don't hurry.* Wait until sickness overtakes you, but don't wait until you become senile. *I and your other loved ones will have prepared a happy welcome for you.* . . .[43]

An example of the third form of reunion reads —

Cause I'm very very lonesome for my wife, brothers and sisters and fear blindness.[44]

Granting that it is not religious prohibitions that prevent suicide and that it is caused by the nature and ordering of the individual's problems, religious teachings may exert a kind of temporary holding effect on the individual. If things do not improve with time, however, any religious prohibition may be resolved by one or another of the alternatives being discussed here.

Oh I know I must be wrong, but if so, why does God let me live? Life is unbearable to me now, and if things don't get better, something happens.[45]

In concluding this discussion of the way in which religion is used to construct the moral justification of suicide, the author hopes that he has demonstrated why the study of the role of morality in suicide is not *an insoluable problem*, nor is it destined to produce *uninstructive data*. In fact, it has already shown every evidence of offering a *law* of considerable interest.

It is peculiar that Durkheim should have believed otherwise. After all, the basis on which we were advised to seek the *causes* of suicide rates (as opposed to the *essential characteristics* of suicide) is that the stability of suicide rates is indicative of some greater underlying truth that will explain the *why* of social suicide rates, if not the *how* of suicide.

> The suicide rate is therefore a factual order, unified and definite, as is shown by both its permanence and its variability. For this permanence would be inexplicable if it were not the result of a group of distinct characteristics, solidary one with another, and simultaneously effective in spite of different attendant circumstances; and this variability proves the concrete and individual quality of these same characteristics, since they vary with the individual character of society itself.[46]

Yet the stability of rates is taken to be a sign of weakness, when it is found in the categories of motives attributed by officials to suicides.[47]

Durkheim goes on to argue the following:

> . . .What are called statistics of motives of suicides are actually statistics of opinions concerning such motives of officials, often of lower officials, in charge of this information service. Unfortunately, official establishments of fact are known to be often defective even when applied to obvious material facts comprehensible to any conscientious observer and leaving no room for evaluation. How suspect must they be considered when applied not simply to recording an accomplished fact, but to its interpretation and explanation! . . .The value of improvised judgements, attempting to assign a definite origin for each special case from a few hastily collected bits of information is, therefore, obviously slight.[48]

Having made much of this point in an attempt to belittle the official designation of motives and their potential to explain the *causes* of suicide rates, Durkheim says nothing of how the *improvised judgments* of officials were any more valid when it came to assigning the cause of death in any particular case to suicide. Certainly, these officials were unaware of Durkheim's definition of suicide. Even if they had been aware of it, one cannot help but wonder on what basis they would have decided who fit the definition. The definition reads, "The term suicide is applied to all cases of death resulting directly or indirectly from a positive or negative act of the victim himself, which he knows will produce this result."[49] In order to make a reasonable choice in assigning the cause of death, it would be required that one be able to establish whether or not ". . .at the moment of the acting the victim knows the certain results of his conduct, no matter what reason may have led him to act thus."[50] We are told that the above may be established by ". . .an easily recognizable feature, for it is not impossible to discover whether the individual did or did not know in advance the natural results of his action."[51] How one went about establishing this easily recognizable feature is an element in the discussion that is conspicuously absent. Indeed, one wonders why it is not impossible to discover whether, at the time of his act, the individual is aware in advance of the outcome of that act (or aware of anything else), if we do as Durkheim repeatedly suggests we do and not concern ourselves with the individual, his motives, or his ideas.

There is a considerable literature on the problem of establishing the individual's intent with respect to the act of suicide.[52] Rather than acknowledge and deal with this problem (especially after he specifically stipulates in the opening of the book that his case rests upon the "scientific" establishment of and adherence to a definition of suicide based upon intent), Durkheim ignores his own definition for the remainder of the book and somehow overlooks the fact that the officials responsible for compiling the statistics on which his work is based have also ignored it.

I have already indicated why I believe a study of the individual's motives and morals is not only useful, but essential in the search for a better understanding of suicide. The data presented in this paper, and its analysis, offers one encouraging way of pursuing such a study. However, it need not be limited to this. It can also provide a means of explaining social suicide rates. The following discussion is intended to caution the reader not to use the author's analysis in this way even if it seems expedient to do so. It may be argued that Durkheim and others concerned with the interpretation of official rates have, in the course of establishing the "legitimacy" of the etiological approach, excluded themselves from another means of succeeding in this undertaking, by placing the study of the individual and his morals, motives, and intentions outside the realm of legitimate inquiry. I referred in the previous sentence to the possibility of *succeeding* in the interpretation of rates. By this I meant that it is possible to make a convincing case for the correspondence found between the rates and certain social phenomena. Such a correspondence and its accompanying explanation constituted for Durkheim the establishment of causes. The author feels that the widespread acceptance of these assumptions and procedures is unfortunate, not only because there are good grounds on which to question the validity of rates, (Are there actual suicides to constitute the statistics representing the rates of suicide given in the categories of age, race, sex, religion, etc.?) but, because it is possible to explain the correspondence found between the rates and any number of social phenomena in an equally convincing manner. Not only is it possible to explain the rates in a variety of ways, but it is impossible, using this approach, to know which, if any, of these alternatives is correct, since there are no grounds outside the interpretation itself by which to resolve such a question.

For example, it is possible, using the author's sources of data and form of analysis, and Durkheim's own arguments, to explain the descending rates of suicide found among Protestants, Catholics, and Jews, but for reasons completely different than Durkheim supposed. To do so required only that we try to view religious teachings not as Durkheim saw them, but as they are seen by the potential suicide. Such a perspective has already been outlined in this paper. By adopting this approach, we can provide a reasonable and consistent alternative to Durkheim's hypothesis and explain why suicide rates range from high to low among Protestants, Catholics, and Jews. Such an explanation would also eliminate the very loose reasoning Durkheim was obliged to resort to in order to resolve the Jewish question. For example, among the three major religions, Jews alone have no specific moral prohibitions against suicide.[53] One needs to infer these prohibitions from the sacredness of life argument. Neither do Jews place much emphasis on the hereafter and Heaven or Hell,[54] yet they are somehow, restrained. Then, too, we are told that, although the Jews are more educated (a condition predisposing to suicide), the nature of their education is different.[55] However, the nature of higher education among Catholics and Protestants is the same.[56] These and many other logical inconsistencies too numerous to list here are not satisfactorily dealt with in Durkheim's argument that it is the relative extent of social integration among Protestants, Catholics, and Jews that is responsible for their suicide rates.

An alternative hypothesis in terms of *moral causitry* can be stated as follows: The potential suicide, whether Catholic, Protestant, or Jew, feels the necessity of killing himself because of the nature, ordering, and severity of his problems as he sees them. In contemplating suicide, he hopes to achieve essentially two ends, if possible: (1) to rid himself of the unbearable burden his life's circumstances have placed upon him and (2) to renew his hope for a better lot in the hereafter. It needs further to be noted that whereas religious prohibitions are not ultimately binding in preventing suicide, the prospect that one will be rid of his current set of problems and achieve a better life in the hereafter is binding and serves to encourage suicide. To the extent that the potential suicide is able, as we have shown, to resolve the moral prohibitions of suicide and at the same time convince himself that he will reap all the benefits of a virtuous Christian dying of natural causes, Judaism holds less promise for future happiness than Catholicism and Protestantism. The Jew, it is true, can "put an end to it all," a prospect that is not unattractive for one who feels that he has suffered so much for so long with the expectation of more to come. It is not surprising that some Jews do commit suicide. However, the prospect that "when you're dead, you're dead" is hardly as attractive as living on forever in Heaven, or even Hell, when it is supposed that Hell promises fewer problems than life or at the very least, the possibility of fewer problems. Protestantism and Catholicism have provided for the explicit prohibition of suicide, through the vehicle of Heaven and Hell. Durkheim's mistake was to suppose that the potential suicide both knew and internalized his religious beliefs and that these beliefs were binding. As previously noted, the potential suicide does not think in this way. As a result, the position of Catholicism and Protestantism from the perspective of the potential suicide is not to discourage, but to encourage suicide at least with respect to the relative effects of Judaism. The gist of this is that religious prohibitions do not prevent suicide; therefore, the fact that Protestants and Catholics are both explicit in their prohibition of it does not per se effect their rates of suicide. This is as Durkheim supposed, but for completely different reasons. However, what does encourage suicide in the suicidal person is his ability to convince himself that he will finally be rid of his present troubles and, at the same time, be able to establish the prospect for a brighter future in the hereafter. In this regard, the promise is greater for Protestants and Catholics than for Jews. While this offers an explanation for why Jews have lower rates than Protestants and Catholics, it does not explain why Catholics have lower rates than Protestants. As Durkheim pointed out, Protestants are more rational and individualistic in their interpretation of their religious beliefs than Catholics. This makes it easier for the Protestant than for the Catholic to accomplish the "rationalization" necessary to convince himself that in death he is about to be rid of his present troubles and to embark upon a better life (the explicit religious prohibitions notwithstanding). Hence, Protestants have a higher suicide rate than Catholics, who have a higher rate than Jews.

The above argument, while it has the advantage of being empirically based and is more consistent and parsimonious than Durkheim's *lack-of-social-integration* interpretation of suicide rates, is not being advocated by the author as an alternative explanation. Rather, it has been presented to show why sociologists would do well to reevaluate the wisdom of seeking a better understanding of social phenomena through the interpretation of official rates. The author has briefly outlined in the course of the paper some of the serious dilemmas one is sure to encounter in applying the etiological approach.[57] An alternative source of data, as well as methodological and theoretical orientation, has been presented by the author in this essay.

The analysis of suicide notes and case history material presented in this paper has shown how suicides and suicide attempters were able, by their own accounts, to use religion to construct the moral justification of suicide. This is a radical position to offer in that it has been generally held that the teachings of Protestantism, Catholicism, and Judaism either all work equally well to prevent suicide or, in the case of Durkheim's argument, have little or no influence on suicide prevention. In order to arrive at the above formulation, the author was obliged from the outset to take the accounts of the suicides seriously. Furthermore, in order to evaluate these accounts, it was necessary to place them within the context of the suicide's past and present situation and future expectations as he related them. The author recommends that such procedures be generally applied to the study of all social phenomena. To exclude the individual, his beliefs, motivations, and intentions from the legitimate concern of sociological inquiry is to exclude the discipline from the means of studying suicide in particular and society in general. Given Durkheim's intentions, I need hardly point out how ironic this would be.

REFERENCES

1. Louis I. Dublin, *Suicide: A Sociological and Statistical Study.* New York, The Ronald Press Company, 1963, p. 101.
2. Ibid., pp. 102-3.
3. Helen Silving, Suicide and law. In Edwin S. Shneidman and Norman L. Farberow (Eds.), *Clues to Suicide.* New York, McGraw-Hill, 1957, p. 80.
4. Emile Durkheim, *Suicide: A Study in Sociology.* New York, The Free Press, 1951, p. 157.
5. Jack Douglas, *The Social Meanings of Suicide.* Princeton, New Jersey, Princeton University Press, 1967, p. 205.
6. Heinrich Zimmer, *Philosophies of India.* New York, Meridian Books, 1957, p. 167.
7. Silving, op. cit., p. 80.
8. Ibid., p. 80.
9. Ibid., p. 80.
10. Dublin, op. cit., pp. 103-4.
11. David Hume, Of Suicide, in Alasdair McIntyre (Ed.), *Hume's Ethical Writings.* New York, Collier Books, 1965, pp. 305-6.
12. Jerry Jacobs, *Adolescent Suicide Attempts: The Culmination of a Progressive Social Isolation,* unpublished doctoral dissertation, Copyright 1967, p. 47. For a more detailed analysis of these aspects, the reader is referred to these additional works of the author:
    1. Joseph D. Teicher and Jerry Jacobs, Adolescents who attempt suicide: Preliminary findings. *American Journal of Psychiatry, 122*(11):1248-1257, 1966.
    2. Joseph D. Teicher and Jerry Jacobs, The physician and the adolescent suicide attempter. *The Journal of School Health, 36*(9):406-415, November, 1966.
    3. Jerry Jacobs and Joseph D. Teicher, Broken homes and social isolation in attempted suicides of adolescents. *The International Journal of Social Psychiatry, 13*(2):139-149, 1967.
13. Ludwig Brinswanger, The case of Ellen West, in Rollo May, et al. (Eds.), *Existence.* New York, Basic Books, 1958, p. 267.
14. One of a set of 112 suicide notes from persons successful in suicide in the Los Angeles area.
15. Ibid.
16. Op. cit., see Footnote 14.
17. W. Morgenthaler and Marianne Steinber, Letzte Aufzeichmungen von Selbstmordern. *Schweiz Z Psychol,* Anwend., 1945, No. 1 p. 150. Forty-seven suicide notes of persons commiting suicide, Case 34-35, in Bern between 1929 and 1935.

18. Genuine and simulated suicide notes, in Edwin S. Shneidman and Norman L. Farberow, *Clues to Suicide*. New York, McGraw-Hill, 1957, p. 209.

19. A youth who was prematurely tired, in Ruth Cavan, *Suicide*. Chicago, University of Chicago Press, 1928, p. 243.

20. James Jan-Tausch, *Suicide of Children: 1960-63, New Jersey Public School Students*. Trenton, New Jersey, New Jersey Dept. of Education, p. 18.

21. D.J. West, *Murder Followed by Suicide*. Cambridge, Harvard University Press, 1966, p. 42.

22. Case Histories of Fifty Adolescent Suicide Attempters completed during Adolescent Suicide Attempt Project, NIMH Grant #1R11MHO1432-02, 1964-1967, University of Southern California School of Medicine, Department of Psychiatry. Co-directed by the author.

23. Ibid.

24. Op. cit., Case Histories.

25. Ibid.

26. Ibid.

27. Op. cit., Marion Blake and her loves, in Ruth Cavan, p. 205.

28. Op. cit., see Footnote 14.

29. Ibid.

30. Op. cit., Case Histories.

31. Op. cit., Genuine and simulated suicide notes, in Shneidman and Farberow, p. 214-215.

32. Op. cit., see Footnote 14.

33. Op. cit., Genuine and simulated suicide notes, in Shneidman and Farberow, p. 213.

34. Op. cit., see Footnote 14.

35. Op. cit., see Footnote 17, Case #17.

36. Ibid., Case #16.

37. Ibid., Case #40.

38. Ibid., p. 1.

39. *San Francisco Chronicle*, October 2, 1967, p. 1.

40. Op. cit., Case Histories.

41. Op. cit., Case Histories.

42. Op. cit., see Footnote 17, Case #9.

43. Op. cit., see Footnote 14.

44. Ibid.

45. Op. cit., Marian Blake and her loves, in Ruth Cavan, p. 200.

46. Durkheim, op. cit., p. 51.

47. Ibid., p. 149.

48. Ibid., pp. 148-9.

49. Ibid., p. 44.

50. Ibid., p. 44.

51. Ibid., p. 44.
52. See for example: Harold Garfinkel, *Studies in Ethnomethodology.* Englewood Cliffs, New Jersey, Prentice Hall, Inc., 1967, pp. 11-18 and pp. 76-104, and Robert E. Litman, et al., Investigations of equivocal suicides. *The Journal of American Medical Association, CXXCIV:*924-929, June 22, 1963.
53. Durkheim, op. cit., p. 170.
54. Ibid., p. 170.
55. Ibid., p. 168.
56. Ibid., p. 168.
57. For a more complete discussion of these problems, the reader is referred to works of Garfinkel, op. cit., pp. 18-24, Harvey Sacks, Sociological description. *Berkeley Journal of Sociology, 8:*1-16, 1963 and op. cit. Douglas.

Chapter 5

HARRY HALLER'S PRIVATE SKY HOOK:
The Role of Suicidal Ideation in
The Prolongation of Life

IN the preceding chapter we have seen how moral justifications serve to justify suicidal ideation and suicidal acts for the would-be suicide. In this chapter we will see how suicidal ideation (thinking about committing suicide) can serve, not only to promote suicide (as is generally believed) but to prolong the life of the potentially suicidal person. How this can happen will be dealt with below.

Abstract

Suicidal ideation is most often dealt with in the literature as being either itself pathological or in some way symptomatic of underlying pathology. At the same time, many authorities hold that while everyone, or nearly everyone, has probably entertained the notion of killing themselves, relatively few persons actually resort to suicide. With this in mind, it seems more reasonable to suppose that suicidal ideation is "normal," i.e. a general condition of society. What's more, since so many entertain suicide and so few accomplish it, it may be that suicidal ideation actually plays some key role in the retardation and/or prevention of suicide. This paper will consider some of the ways in which suicidal ideation may lead to the prolongation of life.

67

Upon addressing the members of the Vienna psychoanalytic society in 1910, Doctor Rudolph Reitler noted, "For most people the impulse (to suicide) is sufficient. In fact, the mere idea that the anxiety can be ended once and for all seems to have such a comforting effect that one almost gets the impression that many people are kept alive only by their suicidal fantasies" (Reitler, 1967, p. 68).

The notion of suicidal threats or ideation, or suicide attempts, sometimes working to help resolve real life problems for the potential suicide and thereby reduce or eliminate the motive for suicide, has received some credence in the literature.* However, by far the greatest bulk of the work in this area has concerned itself with the pathological nature of the above phenomena.† For example, little has been said of the role of suicidal ideation in the prolongation of life. This paper will be concerned with the role of ideation, or more specifically, contractual forms of suicidal ideation and their positive potential for prolonging the life of suicidal persons.

The author will consider three contractual forms of suicidal ideation: (1) contracts negotiated between two or more parties in which all parties are aware of their respective obligations; (2) contracts between two or more parties in which only one party is aware of the others' obligation, whereas the others must infer their obligation to the party of the first part on the basis of prior mutually shared background expectancies (Garfinkel, 1967); and (3) a form of contractual arrangement in which the individual makes a pact with himself. If the notion of one con-

---

*See for example D. Bucove (1968, p. 262) for an instance of suicidal ideation serving as a basis for therapeutic abortion. E. Stengel and N.G. Cook (1958, pp. 120-121) for the positive effects of suicide attempts in resolving – for most of the suicide attempters in Stengel's sample – their problems and with them the motivation to suicide.

†See for example N. Tabachnick and D.I. Klugman (1965, p. 84). In comparing two sets of callers telephoning the Los Angeles Suicide Prevention Center, the authors found – in terms of diagnostic categories – that they were unable to apply to any of a total of sixty-nine callers the category of *no significant pathology*. H.I. Schneer and P. Kay (1961, p. 200) "The wish for sleep, in the suicidal behavior at adolescence, represents a megalomanic method of coping with overwhelming problems of sexual identification, a sense of identity, and handling of aggression, which explosively rids the adolescent of the oedipal struggle" C.W. Wahl (1957, O. 23).

tracting with oneself to prolong one's life seems unusual, contracting with another to this end is common everyday practice. One contracts with the landlord or bank for shelter, with the hospital or physician for medical care, with the police and military for the protection of life and property, i.e. the social contract implicit in the delegation of authority to an institutionalized other, etc. These and other contractual forms of social interaction are negotiated with an eye to improving one's life chances. While none of these contracts constitute per se an instance of suicidal ideation, they may become a form of suicidal ideation if placed in the proper context. The following are some examples.

First Form of Suicidal Ideation

One of the more universal forms of institutionalized contractual arrangements is marriage. It is perhaps not surprising to find when the subjective state of so many of society's members is described by such terms as *powerlessness, normlessness, meaninglessness* (Seeman, 1959), or the *blasé attitude* (Simmel, 1950) that members tend to view marriage as one of the few remaining ways of establishing and perpetuating meaningful social relationships. The need to succeed in this pursuit in order to be able to establish and maintain adequate grounds for living has been dealt with in detail in the author's previous works (Jacobs, 1967; Jacobs and Teicher, 1967). The fact that marriage does not always allow for the realization of this expectation has done little to deter members from marrying. Members often enter into a marriage contract in order to secure (among other things) what they see as one of the few remaining potential sources of loyalty, empathy, or closeness. The destructive influence of the dissolution of a marriage upon the life of either or both parties may, in such cases, be expected to be proportionate to the marriage's constructive influence while still binding. Ropschitz and Ovenstone (1968), in a study of suicide and suicidal threats, noted, "Striving for love and affection, for recognition, self-assertion and dominance, stood in the foreground. Quarrels between spouses, [and] lover's tiffs . . .by far outnumbered any other precipitating cause."

The following excerpt from a long suicide note is characteristic of the message found in many notes recounting the effects of separation situations:

Received the divorce papers today and was astonished by them.... It has been stated that a coward takes his own life. Not completely true. I don't want to do it. In fact, I am plain terrified at the thought. But, as my mother said, when the sweetness of life is gone, there is no further reason to live. . . . It hurts to have to bargain with a third party [the attorney] to speak to one's wife. If one does not have his wife's loyalty, what can he count on, live for? There is nothing left for me to live for (Jacobs, 1967).

Given the high divorce rate in this country, it is not unreasonable to suppose that many persons are subject to a form of suicidal ideation in which the marriage contract figures prominently. Suicidal ideation revolving around the conditions of the marriage may be expected to take one of two forms: persons unhappily married may wish a divorce in order to rectify what either or both see as an unwitting error, i.e. to try again to establish a meaningful social relationship with another, or those who are happily married may feel that they need to perpetuate the marriage and, if unable to, become suicidal. Although either of these two forms is logically possible, the author has only found evidence for the latter in the notes, case histories, and diaries of suicides. The following is an example. The author recently had occasion to hear the case history of a patient who, in addition to the covenant between him and his wife given in the marriage vows, negotiated at the time of his marriage a separate contract with her to remain married for a minimum of five years. The first five years were soon up, and the husband sought to renegotiate the original contract for another five years. The wife refused. The husband felt that without the binding effect of the contract the marriage would not last long, and if it were dissolved, he would not find life worthwhile and would kill himself. Both the patient and the wife attributed their success in staying married for the first five years to the contract. To the extent that the husband held all along that he would kill himself upon the dissolution of the marriage, or conversely, that he had grounds to live and would not kill himself while the marriage continued, the above constitutes a case of contractual form of suicidal ideation being responsible for prolonging the life of a potential suicide. As previously indicated, many suicide notes recount the way in which the continuation of the marriage functioned to perpetuate life, with or without the additional binder of a separate outside contract. The marriage vows are after all, for most, contract enough. Swearing to love, honor, and obey, for better or for worse, till death do you part, leaves little room for ambiguity.

The author does not mean to imply from the above discussion that a marriage contract is per se a form of suicidal ideation. Rather I have tried to point out some of the expectations frequently held by persons entering into marriage, and why it is not uncommon, when the marriage is threatened, for the husband and/or wife to entertain the notion of suicide. The way in which marriage figures in this form of suicidal ideation and the key role it often plays in stopping the individual short of the end of hope (Kobler and Stotland, 1964) is one important example of how a contractual form of suicidal ideation may work to prolong the life of the potential suicide.

Another example of a social contract that takes the form of suicidal ideation and may result in the prolongation of life is the suicide pact. Suicide pacts may take at least one of two basic forms. A recent article in the New York Times is indicative of the first form. It quotes a suicide note (letter) written by a Czech student, the first of a series of Czech citizens to ignite themselves in protest against the Soviet Union's current influence in their country's internal affairs:

With regard to the fact that our nations are at the edge of hopelessness, we decided to express our protest and awaken the people of this country in the following way:

Our group is composed of volunteers who are ready to burn themselves for our cause. I had the honor to draw the first lot and have gained the right to write the first letter and set the first torch.

Our requirements are: (1) Immediate abolition of censorship; (2) Prohibition of distribution of Zpragug (the newspaper published by the Soviet occupation force).

Should our requirements not be fulfilled within five days, that is by January 21, 1969, and if the people will not come out with sufficient support (such as a strike for an indefinite period), further torches will go up in flames (signed Torch No. 1).*

It is clear here (as in the case of the marriage contract) that it remains for the second party, in this case the people or the government, to move Torch No. 2 away from the edge of hopelessness. Suicidal persons, i.e. members of the above group holding to this form of suicidal ideation, will not kill themselves if, from their perspective, the second party does not continue to be in breach of contract. In fact it is stipulated under the terms of the contract that Torch No. 2 may not kill himself, whatever the circumstances, for at least five days. Such a stipulation guarantees Torch No. 2 a minimum of five more days of life. In the event of a settlement, the motive to suicide will have been taken from him entirely and another potential suicide will have been saved by his suicidal ideation.

The above is characteristic of one form of suicide pact. It stands in contrast to the two-party suicide pact usually found in Western industrial societies. In such cases the pact is generally negotiated between two persons, both of whom agree to kill themselves at the same time and in the same place. In the case of the Czech students, two or more persons negotiated to kill themselves, one at a time, five days apart, and in unspecified places. The example of the students is atypical in that this form of suicide pact is usually more characteristic of Eastern nonindustrialized societies, not only with respect to the means of suicide (self-immolation) but also with respect to the fact that the suicides occurred separated in time and space. This form has, however, become more common in Western countries since a series of self-immolations by Vietnamese priests and nuns in protest against the Vietnam war. These two kinds of suicide pacts can be better contrasted if we specify the conditions of the Western variety and cite a comparative example. Its general conditions may be given as follows: (1) two parties agree to kill themselves or, one the other and then

---

*New York Times, January 18, 1969, p. 8.

himself, (2) in each other's presence, (3) often under specified conditions, and (4) at some future time. The need to fulfill all of these conditions works to establish for both parties a problematic outcome for their intended act. For example, since both parties must kill themselves in the presence of the other, and their mutual understanding is that this is to be a reciprocal undertaking, if one reneges, the other, no longer bound, may also renege. (The author has heard several cases of this kind presented by psychiatrists, where a breach of contract by one led to the survival of both parties to the pact. Two adolescent suicide attempters in a prior study by the author also gave such accounts).* Second, in such cases as it is agreed that one party should kill the other and then himself or if each is to kill only himself, and this is not accomplished simultaneously, the one who is last to act may — upon witnessing the death of the first — have second thoughts. If the conditions under which the pact is to be accomplished are specified and these conditions cannot be properly arranged, the attempt may have to be postponed or, if not postponed, attempted by some other means that may allow for the survival of either or both. Last, and perhaps most important, is the fact that the pact is negotiated for some future time. The following are excerpts from the accounts of a teenage girl, who had made a suicide pact with a teenage boy:

I was in one of my depressed moods when I got the urge to take in one dose, the entire bottle of medicine given to me by the doctor when I cut my wrists [on the occasion of a prior attempt]. The bottle was almost half full, I had the empty bottle in my hand and was falling asleep when my Aunt Martha found me and called an ambulance. The hospital used a stomach pump on me and again advised that I see a psychiatrist. My mother promised to send me to one. This time I asked my mother not to. I promised her that I would behave better. However, a week later I was up on the roof of our apartment house looking out over the city and not sure of why I was there when I was startled

*Adolescent Attempted Suicide Study, supported by National Institute of Mental Health Grant 1R11MHO1432-02, conducted at the Los Angeles County General Hospital and co-directed by the author.

to hear a voice behind me. "You're Alice Hurley, aren't you?"
I turned to see a boy about fifteen sitting with his back against
the chimney facing me.

"Who are you?" I asked.

"I'm Peter Curden," replied the boy. "I'm in your history
class at school — were you going to jump?" The last question
somehow startled me.

"No," I denied. "I was just trying to get away from people.
I wanted to be alone. What are you doing here?"

I found Peter to be a very nice boy, the only boy I ever
talked to that made me feel unafraid. We met on the roof many
times and discussed life. . . .

We talked at great length about our reading and about life.
We were in complete agreement that the world was entirely
materialistic and the present goals of man were economic. There
seemed to be no time for true expression of self and enjoyment
of nature. We usually concluded that life as we are forced to live
it is purposeless and that we must either awaken the world to its
true purpose or seek self-destruction. . . .

With Peter, I went in the evening to the home of a teacher,
to whom I thought we might talk about life as we saw it. The
teacher seemed frightened by us and by what we were saying. In
a fit of temper he ordered us out of his home and threatened to
report our behavior to the school principal.

To both Peter and me it seemed as though the last possible
person with whom we might communicate had refused to accept
us as human beings with feelings.

It was late in the evening when we reached my house. We
were too disturbed to want to go to our respective homes so we
went to the roof to talk. There seemed to be no way of reaching
anyone. Communications in this world are limited to the bare
necessities to maintain life and continue on course.

We stayed up very late that night. The more we talked the
more hopeless everything seemed to be. We decided we were
going to communicate in such a way that people couldn't help

but respond. We would commit suicide but, to make sure it would not be in vain we would do it in a dramatic way. We would jump from a high building after we had set the building on fire and attracted a lot of attention.

The next day we met in the cellar of my house where we knew kerosene was stored. Each of us filled a milk bottle with kerosene and placed it in a paper bag. Twenty minutes later we entered the lobby of the largest building in town. Walking past the elevators we entered the stairway and quickly poured the kerosene on the walls and the floor. Then with the bottle still in our hands we ran up the stairway a few steps and put a match to the paper bags. Throwing the burning bags to the floor we raced up the stairway as we heard the fire start. Still clinging to the bottles we mounted the steps to the second, the third, and the fourth floors. By the time we reached the fourth floor the fire had been discovered and we could hear people calling out in alarm. Quickly we mounted the last steps which led to the roof trapdoor. Our plan seemed perfect, and I had a feeling of high exhilaration. Then came catastrophe. The trap door was locked! We looked at each other and without a word we broke the bottles and slashed at our wrists with the sharp glass edges. I watched the blood fall on my dress and on the steps. I was watching the blood flow, completely unconscious of everything about me, when I was seized and carried down the steps. I can't remember anything after that until I awakened in a hospital. I don't know why but when I regained consciousness and saw the nurse sitting next to me I asked one question, "How is Peter?" The nurse's answer sounded so satisfying. "Just five minutes ago, he awoke and asked 'How's Alice?' "

The outcome of the pact was the following:

Both Alice Hurley and Peter Curden spent a month in the hospital after which Alice and her mother moved to another city in New Jersey. Peter went to live with his aunt and uncle in still another city. Both Alice and Peter completed their high school programs successfully. Alice now attends a state college where she is a commuting student and Peter is employed in a large manufacturing plant where he also attends a special training school in the evening (Jan-Tausch, undated).

The above contractual forms of suicidal ideation may be responsible for the perpetuation of the suicidal person's life or, at the very least, make probabilistic his future existence. If one is on the brink of abandoning all hope and views suicide as both imminent and inevitable, then even the latter effect must be viewed as beneficial insofar as the prolongation of life is seen as a preferred outcome.

Second Form

Apart from the contractual forms of ideation in which both parties are aware of their respective obligations, there is a second form of ideation in which the suicidal individual feels there is a binding obligation (or at least hopes so) on the part of a second person, who must for his part infer the existence and/or nature of his obligation to the first on the basis of their prior mutually shared background expectancies.

Mercy killings are an example of this form of suicidal ideation. An individual in the advanced stages of cancer and in great pain, who wants to die and makes his wishes selectively known, might at the very least hope for a spouse or some other person close to him to respect his wishes and murder him. It is commonly understood that mercy deaths constitute equivocal circumstances and a possible exception to the public's general abhorrence of murder and/or suicide. The following suicide note contained in a coroner's report is illustrative: "In the first letter. . .the deceased complained of extreme pain and stated, 'If you receive this letter you will know that I have emptied my bottle of sleeping pills.' The second letter. . .also contained a complaint of pain. . . It concluded 'surely there must be a justifiable mercy death' (*see* Footnote 3). Persons waiting to be delivered often wait a long time. Those who are expected to deliver them are generally found to be one of two sets of persons, i.e. someone with the right or someone with the duty. These are usually God or a spouse or lover, respectively. The following excerpts are examples taken from the diaries of two suicides:

I have just crawled out of bed. Can't sleep. . . . The last rest is all I pray for now. Oh, God, how many times I asked you to take me, take, take me (Cavan, 1928; p. 204).

Life has become a prison camp for me and I long as ardently for death as the poor soldier in Siberia longs for his home- land. . . . It is undignified to live on like this. Karl [her husband], if you love me, grant me death (Binswanger, 1958, p. 258).

Many persons waiting for others to deliver them ultimately end by having to deliver themselves. Both of the above examples are cases in point. Those who hoped that others would respect their wishes to take their lives and end by having to take their own feel that the second party failed them, either because they missed their cue, i.e. they were insensitive and could not appreciate the suicide's situation or because the party or parties of the second part were derelict of duty. However, quite apart from whether or not individuals end by taking their own lives is the fact that even when they do, they do so at a later point than they would have, had they never entertained the notion of a deliverer.

Third Form

The author will now consider the third and final contractual form of suicidal ideation and how it may serve to perpetuate the life of the suicidal person. This discussion will be centered around the person of Harry Haller.* The psychic state of Harry Haller upon the occasion of his forty-seventh birthday (or thereabouts) may be characterized as one of utter despair, nor was this feeling new to him; he was, after all, a Steppenwolf. "He was, infact, as he called himself, a real wolf of the Steppes, a strange, wild, shy – very shy – being from another world. . . . How deep the loneliness into which his life had drifted on account of his dis- position and destiny and how consciously he accepted this lone- liness as his destiny" (p. 4). On contemplating this fate, in the seclusion of his room, and amidst the intimate surroundings of his books, wasted wine bottles, and old cigar butts, Harry resolved to kill himself. However he had made this resolve before, but much to his continued distress, to no avail. While reprehending himself on his former lack of resolve and seeking some way to overcome it, he hit upon the following idea that would on the one hand ensure his success at suicide, and at the same time, prolong a

---

*Harry Haller is the tragic hero of Herman Hesse's novel, *Steppenwolf*, New York, Holt, Rinehart and Winston, 1966.

new and revitalized existence by two years. The old route that had served him and others like him so well would no longer do: "I am curious to see all the same just how much a man can endure. If the limit of what is bearable is reached, I have only to open the door to escape" (p. 49).

In such an ideational form the limit might be reached at any time: tomorrow, next year, or in a decade. It was the ambiguous and unspecified nature of this form of ideation that no longer served Harry as it once did. He needed a new direction, but to have a new direction, you must set out for somewhere new — a new, known, and clearly defined goal. Harry set for this new goal on his fiftieth birthday.

> He appointed his fiftieth birthday as the day on which he might allow himself to take his own life. On this day, according to his mood, so he agreed with himself, it should be open to him to employ the emergency exit or not. Let happen to him what might, illness, poverty, suffering and bitterness, there was a time-limit. It could not extend beyond these few years, months, days whose number daily diminished. And in fact he bore much adversity, which previously would have cost him severe and longer tortures and shaken him perhaps to the roots of his being, very much more easily. When for any reason it went particularly badly with him, when peculiar pains and penalties were added to the desolateness and loneliness and savagery of his life, he could say to his tormentors: "Only wait, two years and I am your master." And with this he cherished the thought of the morning of his fiftieth birthday. Letters of congratulation would arrive, while he, relying on his razor, took leave of all his pains and closed the door behind him. Then gout in the joints, depression of the spirits, and all pains of head and body could look for another victim (pp. 49-50).

Having provided for his death in two years, there was nothing to do in the interim but live. He could not die before, nor could he go on living as he once had since this was the reason for the entire construction in the first place. Thus Harry Haller arrived at a rationalization of life through death and death through life and thereby extended a revitalized existence by two years.

Such a form of suicidal ideation hit upon early in a troubled life, and extended appropriately as needed, would provide that one need not die prematurely by his own hand, and at the same time, allow for the avoidance of the limbo that led to the suicidal ideation in the first place.

The author has outlined three contractual forms of suicidal ideation and discussed the way in which they may serve to perpetuate the potential suicide's life. The author is of the opinion that too little attention has thus far been paid to the positive potential of suicidal ideation in suicide prevention. I am hopeful that this paper will have had some influence on reversing this trend. There is good evidence to suggest that the above forms of suicidal ideation serve for many to delay or prevent suicide.

REFERENCES

Binswanger, L.: The case of Ellen West. In May, R., et al. (Eds.): *Existence.* New York, Basic Books, 1958.

Bucove, D.: A case of pre-partum psychosis and infanticide. *The Psychiatric Quarterly, 42*:262, 1968.

Cavan, R.: Marion Blake and her loves. *Suicide.* Chicago, University of Chicago Press, 1928.

Garfinkel, H.: *Studies in Ethnomethodology.* Englewood Cliffs, New Jersey, Prentice-Hall, 1967, pp. 38-41.

Hesse, H.: *Steppenwolf.* New York, Holt, Rinehart and Winston, 1966.

Jacobs, J.: A phenomenological study of suicide notes. *Social Problems, 15*: 67, 1967.

Jacobs, J., and Teicher, J.D.: Broken homes and social isolation in attempted suicides of adolescents. *International Journal of Social Psychiatry, 13*: 144, 1967.

Jan-Tausch, J.: *Suicide of children: 1960-1963, New Jersey Public School Students.* Bulletin released by the State of New Jersey, Department of Education, pp. 16-17.

Kobler, A.L., and Stotland, E.: *The End of Hope.* New York, Free Press of Glencoe, 1964, p. 252.

Reitler, R.: In Friedman, P. (Ed.): *On Suicide.* New York, International Universities Press, 1967.

Ropschitz, D.H., and Ovenstone, I.M.K.: A two years' survey on self-aggressive acts, suicides and suicidal threats in Halifax district between 1962 and 1964. *International Journal of Social Psychiatry, 14*:173, 1968.

Schneer, H.I., and Kay, P.: The suicidal adolescent. In Lorand, S., and Schneer, H.I. (Eds.): *Adolescents: Psychoanalytic Approach to Problems and Therapy.* New York, Paul B. Hoeber, 1961, p. 200.

Seeman, M.: On the meaning of alienation. *American Sociological Review, 24*:783-791, 1959.

Simmel, G.: The metropolis and mental life. In Wolff, K.H. (Ed.): *The Sociology of George Simmel.* Glenco, The Free Press, 1950, pp. 409-424.

Stengle, E., and Cook, N.G.: *Attempted Suicide*. London, Chapman & Hall, 1958, pp. 120-121.

Tabachnick, N., and Klugman, D.I.: No name — A study of anonymous suicidal telephone calls. *Psychiatry, 28*:84, 1965.

Wahl, C.W.: Suicide as a magical act. In Shneidman, E.S., and Farberow, N.L. (Eds.): *Clues to Suicide*. New York, McGraw-Hill, 1957, p. 23.

Chapter 6

MANIC DEPRESSION AND SUICIDE

WE have contended throughout this work that suicide is better understood as a conscious rational (rather than an unconscious irrational) act. It has generally been held that the act of killing one's self does not imply mental illness or symptoms of mental illness. However, this is not to say that some people who commit suicide are not diagnosed by psychiatrists (or others) as being mentally ill. Indeed, adolescent suicide attempters are often diagnosed as schizophrenic.

We will be concerned in this chapter with manic depression and suicide and whether or not the timing of suicides and suicide attempts among this group of persons conforms to a rational or irrational pattern of behavior.

One better known monograph in the suicide literature is entitled *The End of Hope* (Kobler and Stotland, 1964). It describes the way in which a new and well meaning administrator of an inpatient psychiatric unit inadvertently succeeds in defining the patients' condition as worse than it is. By doing so, he creates in the patients a feeling characterized by *the end of hope*. In fact, this theme is the leitmotif of a considerable literature on the topic of suicide. What this means is that insofar as life is defined by the folk concept, "full of ups and downs," one lives in the expectation that anything can happen. This in turn provides for hope, and at the very least, a potentially rosier future. It is only when the individual succeeds on the basis of his past experiences in defining the world as not full of ups and downs, only downs, that one

encounters the end of hope. Many such persons experience suicidal ideation and typically reach out in a cry for help (Farberow
and Shneidman, 1965).

In this paper, we will consider a set of persons for whom a
world characterized by ups and downs is nonproblematic. Such
persons should be unlikely candidates for suicide since there is no
question of an end of hope. While one would expect the life
chance of such individuals to be very good with respect to the
question of suicide, the statistics indicate otherwise. It has long
been noted that suicide is frequent among manic depressives
(Zilboorg, 1937) and suicide attempts even more common (Fieve,
1975). The question is: Why should this be? Given what we have
just said, there would appear to be a contradiction in that either
there is something wrong with the ups-and-downs theory, or there
is something wrong with the statistics. That the theory can be well
defended is evidenced in many quarters (Jacobs, 1971, 1967,
1976; Kobler and Stotland, 1964; Cavan, 1928). Jacobs (1967)
has noted that it is only when the individual perceived that life is
not full of ups and downs that the end of hope occurs and one
experiences the onset of suicidal ideation. Previously unreported
data within Glassner's (1978) study has indicated that among
manic depressives, what allows the individuals to tolerate the
manic stage is the view that the depressive stage is sure to follow,
and what allows them to tolerate the depressive stage is their
belief in the inevitable coming of the manic stage (cf. Fieve, 1975;
Arieti, 1974). Here we see life full of ups and downs in the extreme. Indeed, manic depressives tend to formulate this saving
cycle as an ideal type. Participant observations on psychiatric
wards reveal psychiatric nurses, aides, and psychiatrists anticipating and predicting for one another, and for the patients, the dates
upon which particular patients will swing from depression to
mania or vice versa. These observations of professional persons
lend further support for the contention that not only the manic
depressives but the professionals believe these shifts to be inevitable. The dominance of lithium as the drug of choice for manic
depression is also founded upon this notion of inevitable mood
swings.

Allowing that there is substance to the theory obliges us to check the statistics found in the literature, which says that manic depressives frequently attempt and at high rates succeed at suicide. We will attempt an explanation of this apparent discrepancy within the context of the ups-and-downs theory.

It should be noted at the outset that our comments apply, however, not only to the ups-and-downs theory in its most basic form, but in elaboration as well. Thus, Farberow (1968) notes that the collective conclusion of psychological research on suicide is that the typical suicide will reveal all or most of the following characteristics: (1) ambivalence about life and death, (2) feelings of hopelessness, (3) feelings of physical or psychological exhaustion, (4) feelings of unrelieved anxiety, tension, depression, anger, or guilt, (5) feelings of chaos with inability to restore order, (6) mood swings, (7) inability to see alternatives, (8) loss of interest in usual activities, and (9) physical distress. With the possible exceptions of Items, 1, 7, and 9, these items are found on the standard list of regularly present symptoms of manic depression (Feighner, 1972). Since most manic depressives never kill themselves, we must conclude that the presence of these conditions per se cannot predict suicide. We would argue that suicide occurs only when these conditions combine to produce the unique phenomenon referred to here as the end of hope. The above list (and the fact that manic depressives are subject to most of the items on it) indicates something else as well — that manic depressives are not unlike other persons who commit suicide. As will become evident below, this is an important point with respect to our particular application of the general ups-and-downs theory to manic depression and suicide.

Suicide and Suicide Attempters

One may mean many things by the word *suicide*. The psychiatric literature frequently considers the causes of suicide to stem from unconscious (Stengel, 1964; Tabachnick, 1957), irrational (Stengel and Cook, 1958; Balser and Masterson, 1959), impulsive (Lourie, 1966), or maladaptive (Faberow, 1968; Stengel and Cook, 1958) forms of behavior. Early childhood trauma and frustration-aggression models also figure prominently as causes.

We have already taken issue with some of these notions in Chapter 2. A more detailed treatment follows below.

Unconscious motivation is a difficult position to maintain logically or empirically. Apart from the logical inconsistencies noted in Chapter 2 (inherent in the definition of suicide), of one unconsciously-intentionally taking one's life, there is Jacobs' (1971, 1967) empirical evidence from interviews with suicide attempters seen within forty-eight hours of the attempt (and within suicide notes and diaries of successful suicides) that the victim seems to be always conscious of his intentions prior to the act. Indeed, they tell us they have given the matter a good deal of consideration and have reluctantly come to accept suicide as the only way out. This same data suggests that suicide is not an irrational act. None of the attempters were diagnosed as suffering from thought disorders. Jacob Tuckman et al. (1969) report that they were "impressed with the possibility that in a number of cases suicide could have resulted from a conscious, 'rational' decision reached by weighing the pros and cons." R.W. Parnell and I. Skottowe (1967) found that "from the preventative point of view, the most significant finding is the small number of (suicidal) patients showing disorders of thinking." There is also the more general problem of practitioners' criteria for ascertaining rationality and irrationality. In a study of Rosenhan (1973) it is the rational researchers who were considered irrational by the psychiatric practitioners with whom they interacted. Only the other patients, "the insane," recognized the sanity and rationality of the researchers.

Impulsivity is similarly problematic. As David Hume (1783) noted, "such is our natural horror of death, that small motives will never be able to reconcile us to it." Equally fundamental is the definitional problem noted earlier (in Chapter 2): How can suicide be impulsive if it must be intentional (intentionality implies conscious deliberation)? Impulsive, you will recall was the *sudden inclination to act without conscious thought.*

That suicide *must be* intentional is noted in Durkheim's (1951) definition as well:

The common quality of all these possible forms of supreme renunciation is that the determining act is performed advisedly; that at the moment of acting the victim knows the certain result of his conduct, no matter what reason may have led him to act thus. . . .

We may then say conclusively: the term suicide is applied to all cases of death resulting directly or indirectly from a positive or negative act of the victim himself, which he knows will produce this result (p. 44).

Suicide viewed as a conscious, rational choice is also consistent with the considerable literature indicating that suicidal persons try to communicate their intentions to others in "a cry for help." Suicide as an impulsive act seems both a contradiction in terms and contrary to fact.

Adaptive vs. Maladaptive

In order for suicide to be considered *adaptive or maladaptive*, at least two questions must be taken into account. First, what kinds of adaptive techniques did the victim invoke and in what order? Second, to what were they required to adapt? Case studies found in the psychiatric or psychological literature are not very helpful in answering these questions. Merton J. Kahne (1966) in reviewing the medical literature's concern with the life situations of suicides, notes, "there are occasional, marginal references to the importance of certain aspects of milieu organization as it might relate to patient suicide. On the whole, however, medical literature characteristically leaves the social arrangements and environmental conditions unintegrated with its general explanation of human suicide." Literature on the life events of suicides is more informative. Jacobs (1971) asked, do suicides invoke different sets of adaptive techniques and in a different order than nonsuicides and/or are they required to adapt to a different and more severe set of real life circumstances? His findings indicate that the answers to these questions are "no" to the former and "yes" to the latter. In a formal sense, adolescent suicide attempters invoke adaptive techniques ranging from least to most drastic, in that order, to deal with their problems — the same order used by a control sample of normal adolescents. The difference that accounted for suicide attempters to more often invoke more drastic techniques was determined by what they were asked to adapt to. This is consistent with Paykel's (1974) findings, in his study of fifty-three suicide attempters, fifty-three depressives, and a control group of fifty-three persons from the general population. Using standard life events instruments, Paykel finds that "suicide attempters report more events than general population subjects in almost every category except that of desirable events." Compared to depressives, the suicide's events were more threatening and more often outside the person's control.

Notions of suicide as a conscious, rational, and adaptive choice within a life that has become unbearable go back at least to Plato, who accepted the general proscription against suicide, but listed as exceptions extreme distress, poverty, or affliction. Epicurus, the Stoics, Seneca, and Epictetus all held variations on the position that when life ceases to hold pleasure and hope, a reasonable remedy for free men is to end it. Montesquieu, in admiring the Roman views on suicide, expressed in romantic terms the nature of intentionality in suicide. He described suicide as giving "everyone the liberty of finishing his part on the stage of the world, in what scene he pleased" (Williams, 1967).

The counter view of the irrational, unconscious suicide has its roots in the Christian tradition of Augustine and Thomas Aquinas — that suicide is wrong because the opportunity for penitence is lost, suicide violates natural law, the suicide deprives society of his activity, and the suicide plays God. The modern, medical version of this argument holds that the opportunity for cure is lost, that only a sick personality could violate the natural (Darwinian) law of self-preservation, and that the physician has the duty to keep persons alive, for their own benefit and for the benefit of society.

Suicide and Suicide Attempts

Thus far, we have not distinguished between suicides and suicide attempters, a distinction that is often made in the literature (Mintz, 1964; Stengel and Cook, 1958). This distinction ignores the dimension of intentionality that we are emphasizing. Once one recognizes that all forms of suicide involve intentionality, the distinction between attempts and successes becomes insignificant.

What become important distinctions are the intentions involved in the spectrum of suicidal behaviors. *Lethality scales* attempt to get at this dimension by inferring one's intentionality by the seriousness of self-inflicted injuries. It is assumed, in a manner of speaking, that larger caliber guns indicate larger caliber intentions. Unfortunatley, such items as marital status, sex, degree of planning the technical means to suicide, mode of suicide, telling others, or the use of public and private places for the attempt may have little to do with one's intentions. Then, too, the items on one lethality scale are not found on others, and more generally, lethality scales cannot reliably measure salience, meaning, and other interpretive processes that are changing under various subcultural, historical, and other environmental conditions. These scales may be predictive of static group rates, but are often used to anticipate or retrospectively reconstruct the intentions of individuals — an application for which they are inappropriate. That a potential suicide is white, married, female, poor, uneducated, and Jewish is no indication of her lack of intent to commit suicide, although all of these characteristics correlate inversely with high suicide rates. Such individuals, as noted above, do kill themselves, and any adequate theory of suicide must account for such persons.

Manic Depression and Suicide Statistics

Given our defense of the ups-and-downs theory, one would anticipate that manic depression would actually protect one from suicide. As previously noted, the rates indicate otherwise. We must now look for sources of the lack of goodness of fit between the theory and the rates. In particular, we will look at the ways in which the rates of suicide for manic depressives are generated. It may be, just as suicide and suicide rates for nonmanic depressives are problematic (Jacobs, 1971; Douglas, 1967), so the rates of suicide for manic depressives are also problematic.

Douglas (1967) disputes the Durkheimian's assumptions that there is little systematic bias in suicide statistics, or that these biases are randomly distributed. Douglas cites five sources of systematic bias:

1. Unreliability resulting from the choice of the official statistics to be used in making the tests of the sociological theories.

2. Unreliability resulting from subcultural difference in the attempts to hide suicide.

3. Unreliability resulting from the effects of different degrees of social integration on the official statistics keeping.

4. Unreliability resulting from significant variations in the social imputation of motives.

5. Unreliability resulting from better collection of statistics among certain populations.

Jacobs (1971) deals with this question from a slightly different perspective. According to Durkheim (1951), "in order to proceed with the scientific study of suicide it was first necessary to carefully define it, and having done so, deal only with those cases the definition allowed for." However, Durkheim does not heed his own advice. Excluded from his own definition (quoted previously) are all other acts "in which the victim is either not the author of his own end or else only its unconscious author." It should be clear that in deriving his definition, suicide was based upon considerations of intentionality. Equally clear is the way in which Durkheim completely ignored this basic construction in the remainder of his book. At no point does he seek to establish the intentionality of any of the persons comprising his official rates, nor has he any way of knowing how many of those persons representing the official rates were sane or insane, i.e. capable of intentional acts, or among the sane how many were suicides (cf., Halbwachs, 1930). Certainly the officials responsible for determining the causes of death, while compiling their statistics, statistics upon which Durkheim's work was based, were not referring to his definition when making their designations. How are we (or the Durkheimians) to know what percentage of persons registered as suicides fit Durkheim's and others' definitions of suicide as an intentional act?

Just as the official statistics for suicide generally are problematic, so those for manic depressives may be problematic as well. In addition to the general sources of biases, there are confounding factors when one deals with statistics for manic depressives. As is well known, manic depressives during the manic phase become grandiose and especially active, seeking risks and adventures they would not ordinarily undertake; this may result in accidental deaths that are recorded as suicides. In other cases that Glassner has found among his interviewees, some manics try to level themselves in order to continue at their jobs and do so by combining alcohol, over-the-counter drugs, and physicians' prescriptions (cf., Fieve, 1975). By taking such toxic mixtures inadvertently, another form of accidental death can result that appears to be suicide. Both during mania and depression, persons may cry for help in the form of suicidal gestures dramatic in nature. These cries for help may miscarry and result in death. During depression, many persons are maintained on drugs to counteract the depression. When combined with other drugs or alcohol, these may inadvertently result in death. A feature of depression is the narrowing of focus and inability to recognize alternatives, with fixation on thoughts of the past. During such periods, even in the absence of suicidal ideation, inadequate attention may be given to routine activities, such as driving, walking, or the storage and preparation of foods, resulting in lethal accidents. Although lethal accidents occur among all groups, such accidents occurring among persons with manic depressive histories are more likely to be chalked up as suicides.

Manic Depression and Suicide

We have argued that the ups-and-downs theory for the maintenance of life is reasonable both in scientific terms and in terms of folk wisdom. The suicide statistics for manic depression are, on the other hand, open to skepticism. In the remainder of the paper, we will propose an alternative hypothesis regarding the relationship between manic depression and suicide.

A traditional assumption has been that people commit suicide when they are depressed. A variety of observers have questioned this assumption. Zilboorg (1937) noted, "A number of suicides occur when the depressed person appears to be convalescing and all but recovered from his depressed state." Alex D. Porkony

(1966) summarized, "The individual cases were evaluated in terms of the symptoms of depression at the time of the original consultation. It is apparent there is an inverse relationship here with the slightly depressed having a much higher rate (of suicide) than the seriously depressed." Tuckman, et al., (1969), analyzing the emotional states of suicides through a study of 165 suicide notes, conclude that most were characterized by positive or neutral affect. In the classic example, the case of Ellen West, the husband of a patient of Ludwig Binswanger noted that the day before her death was the only day in years in which she was truly happy.

It would seem, then, that manic depressives would not commit suicide during true depression, since persons generally do not do this. They are further protected from suicide during depression because they anticipate a manic phase to follow. Nor would they likely commit suicide during mania because they would anticipate continuation of cycles. In general, we would suggest that the manic depressive *qua* manic depressive is unlikely to commit suicide.

In light of this, we are led to believe that many persons diagnosed manic depressive who commit or attempt suicide were not at the time of the act actively manic depressive. Data from Glassner's study indicates that while many of the persons he studied had "attempted suicide," few or none had intended to die. Our hypothesis is that persons diagnosed manic depressive, like anyone else, commit suicide only when confronted with the end of hope. The specific conditions under which this can occur for manic depressives are (1) when depressive or manic, one is led to believe that the cycle will not continue or (2) ironically, when one is no longer manic depressive (i.e. when "cured" or normothymic). There are a number of ways in which a manic depressive may become convinced that the other end of the mood swing will not emerge. During the first episode, having never experienced the second stage of the cycle, they may disbelieve the psychiatric staff who predict its onset, which may result in suicide. In other cases, data within Glassner's research suggest that among several patients, when one end of the cycle becomes longer in duration than usual or expected, suicidal behavior often ensues. An illustration of the second condition, "cure" or normothymia, Glassner came across when he was called to give evidence for a psychological autopsy. Half of the manic depressives Glassner had studied had suicide histories, but only this one person had actually died. Glassner looked through this patient's records and the interviews he had with the patient, the patient's family, and physicians and discovered that this patient had been released from the hospital as normothymic only two days before the suicide.

Conclusion

In light of the above discussion, we would recommend a more detailed study of the circumstances surrounding the suicide or suicide attempts of persons who have been diagnosed manic depressive. In light of the ups-and-downs theory of life, one might expect to find that suicide, as defined in this paper, is most likely when manic depressives believe that continuation of the cycle is not forthcoming, or when they become normothymic.

REFERENCES

Arieti, Silvano: Affective disorders. In Arieti, S., and Brody, E. (Eds.): *American Handbook of Psychiatry*. New York, Basic Books, 1974.

Balser, B.H., and Masterson, J.F.: Suicide in adolescents. *American Journal of Psychiatry, 116*(5):400-404, 1959.

Cavan, Ruth S.: *Suicide*. Chicago, University of Chicago Press, 1928.

Douglas, Jack D.: *The Social Meanings of Suicide*. Princeton, Princeton University Press, 1967.

Durkheim, Emile: *Suicide*. New York, Free Press, 1951.

Farberow, Norman L.: Suicide: Psychological aspects. In David Sills (Ed.): *International Encyclopedia of Social Sciences*. New York, Macmillan, 1968.

Farberow, Norman L., and Shneidman (Eds.): *The Cry for Help*. New York, McGraw-Hill, 1965.

Feighner, J., Robins, E., Guze, S., et al.: Diagnostic criteria for use in psychiatric research. *Archives of General Psychiatry, 26*:57-63, 1972.

Fieve, Ronald R.: *Moodswing: The Third Revolution in Psychiatry*. New York, Basic Books, 1975.

Glassner, Barry: Role loss and working class manic depression. Paper presented at the annual meetings of the Society for the Study of Social Problems, 1978.

Halbwachs, Maurice: *Les Causes du Suicide.* Paris, Alcan, 1930.

Hume, David: Of suicide. In Alasdair MacIntyre (Ed.): *Hume's Ethical Writings* (1965). New York, Collier Books, 1783.

Jacobs, Jerry: A phenomenological study of suicide notes. *Social Problems,* 15(1):60–72, 1967.

Jacobs, Jerry: *Adolescent Suicide.* New York, Wiley Interscience, 1971.

Jacobs, Jerry: Suicide: An end to alienation. In Bryce-LaPorte, R. (Ed.): *Alienation and Contemporary Society.* New York, Praeger, 1976.

Kahne, Merton J.: Suicide research: A critical review of strategies and potentialities of mental hospitals. *International Journal of Social Psychiatry,* 12:120–129, 1966.

Kobler, Arthur L., and Stotland, Ezra: *The End of Hopé.* New York, Free Press, 1964.

Lourie, R.A.: Clinical studies of attempted suicide in childhood. *Clinical Proceedings of Children's Hospital of the District of Columbia,* 22:163–173, 1966.

Mintz, R.S.: *A Pilot Study of the Prevalence of Persons in the City of Los Angeles Who Have Attempted Suicide.* Unpublished manuscript presented in summary at the American Psychiatric Association meetings, May, 1964.

Parnell, R.W., and Skottowe, I.: Toward preventing suicide. *Lancet,* 1967, pp. 206–208.

Paykel, Eugene S.: Life stress and psychiatric disorder. In Dohrenwend, B.S., and Dohrenwend, B.P. (Eds.): *Stressful Life Events: Their Nature and Effects.* New York, Wiley, 1974.

Porkony, Alex D.: A follow-up study of 618 suicidal patients. *The American Journal of Psychiatry,* 10:1114, 1966.

Rosenhan, D.L.: On being sane in insane places. *Science,* 179:250–258, 1973.

Stengel, Erwin: *Suicide and Attempted Suicide.* Baltimore, Penguin Books, 1964.

Stengel, Erwin, and Cook, Nancy: *Attempted Suicide.* London, Chapman and Hall, 1958.

Tabachnick, Norman: Observations on attempted suicide. In Shneidman, E.S., and Farberow, N.L. (Eds.): *Clues to Suicide.* New York, McGraw-Hill, Inc., 1957.

Tuckman, Jacob, Kleiner, Robert J., and Lavell, Martha: Emotional content of suicide notes. *American Journal of Psychiatry,* July, 1969, p. 61.

Williams, Granville: Suicide. In Edwards, Paul (Ed.): *The Encyclopedia of Philosophy.* New York, Macmillan, 1967.

Zilboorg, G.: Consideration on suicide. *American Journal of Orthopsychiatry,* 7:15–31, 1937.

Chapter 7

ADOLESCENT SUICIDE ATTEMPTERS

W E have seen in the first six chapters how suicide is a conscious rational act and how moral justifications are necessary to support such an undertaking from the perspective of the potential suicide. These works have incorporated various sources of data: suicide notes, writings found in Belle Lettres, intuitive understanding, the author's subjective experiences, and reference to supporting data taken from a comparative life history study of adolescent suicide attempters.

The concluding chapters, Chapters 7, 8, and 9, will be based primarily upon the author's study of adolescent suicide attempters. This work is linked to the previous chapters through its continued concern with the rational nature of suicidal behavior and thought processes. In particular it will deal with (1) the nature of adolescent and parent interactions, their different perceptions of the same events, and the consequent effect upon the adolescent suicide attempter; (2) a consideration and refutation of the role of broken homes in predisposing one to suicide or depression in later life; and (3) the role of the physician in the life of the would-be suicide during their cry for help.

Adolescents Who Attempt Suicide:
Preliminary Findings

This preliminary paper deals with the conscious rational deliberations of adolescent suicide attempters and the process by which they are led to conclude that death is the only way out.[1]

The Problem

Adolescent suicides and suicidal attempts are a social and medical problem of significant proportions. Of the total number of reported suicides in the U.S. in 1962, 659 individuals were less than twenty years old. Suicide ranks fourth as a cause of death in the fifteen to nineteen age group, surpassed only by accidents, neoplasms, and homicides. Estimates of the ratio of attempted suicides to actual suicides range from 5:1 to 50:1. A review of the vital statistics of 1959 for the U.S. indicates that successful suicide was infrequent under ten years of age, more frequent in the ten- to fourteen-year-old group, and distinctly increased in the fifteen- to nineteen-year-old group.

The trend in death rates by reason of suicide has remained relatively stable since 1950 for females, but rates for males have increased with considerable regularity from the rate of 3.49 deaths per 100,000 in 1950. In the United States suicides accounted for 2.5 percent of all deaths in the age group fifteen to nineteen in 1950, but for 4.3 percent of all deaths in 1962.

According to Louis Dublin,[1] nonfatal suicide attempts occur seven to eight times more frequently than fatal ones. Data are probably inaccurate, for many cases are concealed by parents and physicians as accidents. In contrast to the higher incidence of suicide among adolescent males, there is apparently a higher incidence of suicidal attempts among adolescent females.

In 1960, almost 10 percent of the admissions to the children's and adolescents' services at Bellevue Hospital, New York City, were for suicide attempts or threats. At Kings County Hospital, Brooklyn, a rate of thirteen per 100 admissions was reported for a two-year period. At the Los Angeles County General Hospital, one of the largest in the world and serving a population of over 5 million people, there are about seven adolescents between the ages of fourteen and eighteen admitted each month for an unmistakable suicide attempt.

In the authors' opinion, it is not enough to dismiss a suicide attempt as: (1) an impulsive act; (2) a crisis situation resulting from a temporary upset, where each suicidal episode is considered as an independent event; (3) an insincere gesture, i.e. death is not intended[3]; or (4) an act for which the individual is not responsible or he would not have elected to do as he did[2]; nor (5) need the suicide attempt result from a restricted view of alternatives stemming from a depression.[2] Indeed, an analysis of the data thus far collected in this study through interviews with the adolescent suicide attempters and their parents, an analysis of therapy session tape recordings, suicide notes, unsolicited letters received from the parents following the interviews, and attitudinal data from questionnaires gravely question these views so prevalent in much of the literature.

It is our finding that in the great majority of cases the suicide attempt is considered in advance and, from the perspective of the one who attempts suicide, is weighed rationally against other alternatives and selected over them only after more conventional techniques at solving a progressively serious series of problems have failed, e.g. rebelling, withdrawal, running away from home, physical violence, or psychosomatic complaints. At this point, suicide (where death is intended in the attempt but does not result) or the "suicide attempt" (where only an attention-getting device is intended) is perceived by the adolescent as the only possible solution to his problems.

It is not surprising to find that a high percentage of suicides have "previously threatened or attempted to take their own lives."[5] More often than not adolescents who adopt the drastic measure of an "attempt" as an attention-getting device find that this too fails to open an avenue to a possible solution to their problems. In fact, it generally works to make matters worse. The adolescent is then convinced, or soon becomes convinced, that death is the only solution to what appears to him as the chronic problem of living.

The Sample

The sample consists of adolescents between the ages of fourteen and eighteen who were treated at the Los Angeles County General Hospital for an attempted suicide and who were single, not visibly pregnant, or mentally retarded. The last two criteria were invoked because the mentally retarded could not successfully complete the questionnaires and interviews, and those visibly pregnant were excluded by regulation from the adolescent ward of the LACGH Psychiatric Unit. Records were kept on all teenage suicide attempt patients, but since participation in the study was on a voluntary basis, not everyone treated took part in the study.

From January 1964 through December 1964, sixty-eight adolescents who had attempted suicide were seen by the adolescent attempted suicide project staff. All interviews with parents of these adolescents were conducted at the hospital as well. Forty-eight of these, seen from January through August, are not considered in the following statistical description of the sample. The insight and data gained from interviewing these adolescents and their parents were useful in deciding the final theoretical perspective to be adopted in the study. This pilot group also provided invaluable aid in designing and pretesting the instruments for data collection.

Thus, the data in this paper are based on the twenty cases in the research series, which were studied between September 1964 and mid-January 1965. Three-fourths of these patients were female and the average age was sixteen years. Sixty-two percent were white, twenty-one percent Negro and seventeen percent Mexican-American. Thirty percent of these adolescents came from families in the poverty category, i.e. less than $2700 annual family income.

It is noteworthy that if the other forty-eight had been included, judging from the interviews and case records, the basic statistical data would not have been appreciably altered. All sixty-eight cases were exceedingly homogeneous from the standpoint of having excessive family conflict, broken homes, lack of meaningful social relationships, a history of serious troubles, previous suicide attempts, and some insurmountable problem at the time of the attempt. They all experienced the feeling that this last insurmountable problem, i.e. the "precipitating event," caused the disintegration of any remaining meaningful social relationships.

Procedure

The study is multidisciplinary; psychiatry, sociology, psychology, and medicine are represented. The methodological techniques used by the staff were varied and designed to discern the perspectives of the adolescent and his parent with respect to five major areas of interest: (1) the suicide attempt, (2) family relations, (3) peer group relations, (4) attitudes toward and performance in school, and (5) career aspirations.

The total study sample consisted of fifty adolescents. Indepth interviews with adolescents and parents (usually mothers), attitudinal questionnaires, a battery of psychological tests, and evaluations of the medical status of the adolescent were used to investigate these five major areas. The interview and questionnaire each required about one and one-half hours to complete. The parental interview included questions on the developmental history of the child. Both parent and adolescent were asked identical questions in the areas of *behavioral problems* and *disciplinary techniques* to detect discrepancies in perception.

On the basis of these structured interviews, case histories were constructed according to a standard format covering the five areas listed above. These formed, essentially, two separate stories: the adolescent's biography as told by the parent and the adolescent's autobiography. An attempt was thus made to place the data in the context of the adolescent's total biography where particular attention could then be directed not only to the events, but, more significantly, to their sequential ordering. Information received from suicide notes, unsolicited letters from parents after the interview that related to the home life and the adolescent, an analysis of therapy session tape recordings, and outside information from official sources or from significant others were also used when available.

The study design includes, as well, a control group of fifty nonsuicidal adolescents to be matched as closely as possible on the following: age, race, sex, and socioeconomic status. This group of adolescents and their parents (the matched pairs) will complete the same questionnaires and interviews as did the experimental group, minus the section on the suicide attempt. A complete evaluation of this aspect of the study will be included later in the final data analysis.

Discussion and Analysis of the Preliminary Data

The time, place, and circumstances of any particular suicide attempt may, in some cases, be considered spontaneous, i.e. it occurred to the adolescent at that instant to attempt suicide. However, in a larger view, one must place the notion of spontaneity or an impulsive act from the forefront to the background as a description of the individual's will, or lack of it, at the time of the attempt. Two-thirds of all attempted suicides studied thus far have a history of previous suicide attempts; all of them at the time of the attempt or at some previous time seriously considered suicide as a solution to their problems; 44 percent have had a relative or close friend who attempted suicide or committed suicide; and in one-fourth of these cases a suicide has been attempted by the mother or father.

Relatively few persons attempt suicide in times of crisis, even though it is not surprising to find that many consider suicide under such conditions. In a pretest of the suicide section of the questionnaire given to sixty-eight freshmen in a Southern California college where the average age was seventeen and one-half, 25 percent of this class agreed or strongly agreed with the statement, "I have from time to time seriously considered death as a reasonable solution for some of the problems I have had; for example, as a way to get even with someone, make them feel sorry, leave my worries behind, show them how much I really love them, or to make life easier for someone else."

It is not uncommon to find in the literature that persons attempting suicide are thought to act irrationally.[2, 7] The authors feel this view is unwarranted and that those attempting suicide do not necessarily lack a usual or normal mental clarity or coherence. If one excludes previous suicide attempts, the large majority of adolescents seen by our staff have no previous history of irrational acts and have been viewed by parents, siblings, peers, and teachers as functioning in a rational manner. To regard these rational youths as suddenly irrational exclusively on the basis of the suicide attempt is not, in the author's opinion, merited.

However, the suicide attempt functions to produce exactly this effect on the parents, significant others, peers, and general public — in fact, on almost everyone except the adolescents themselves. This is not surprising because persons who don't attempt suicide have seen no adequate reason to do so. What is left unsaid, of course, is that they see no adequate reason to do so because they do not share the "definition of the situation"[6] held by the suicidal person. The reason for this lack of "reciprocity of standpoints and relevances"[4] is the difference between past and present sets of experiences for the two groups.

The pessimistic world view of the adolescent who attempts suicide is primarily a result of a life characterized by a series of serious problems that erupt unpredictably. These problems, in turn, cause unexpected conflicts, which by their very nature are not given to any resolution known to or tried by the adolescent. Reading an entire case history or, in some instances an auto-biographical suicide note, helps one understand the adolescent's perspective and how he came to embrace a view of the future characterized by the expression *no chance.*

Part of a suicide note that follows (the entire letter was too lengthy to include) illustrates some of the problems faced by the adolescent, how he attempted to cope with them and failed, and finally, how the prospect of suicide emerges as the only solution. The letter was written by a seventeen-year-old Negro male patient to his father the evening before a second suicide attempt was made:

Dear Father,

I am addressing you these few lines to let you know that I am fine and everyone else is and hope you are the same. Daddy I understand I let you down and I let mother down in the same way when I did that lil ole thing (the suicide attempt) that Wednesday night. Daddy I am sorry if I really upset you, but Daddy after I got back I realized how sad and bad you felt when I came back to California, but Daddy I am not happy out here and I'm not happy down there. I just didn't know what to do. I had lost my best girl a week before I did that. I had a fight because some dude tried to take advantage of her when I split to the store so I came back and I heard a lot of noise like bumping so I goes on in and there he is trying to rape my girl and my best one too. So we had a little hassel and he came back with some of his friends you know to get me. So I called up some of my friends and they got to fighting and pretty soon it just turned into slaughter and so a few days later I lost my girl. Her best girlfriend wanted me but I didn't want her so she told Diane a whole bunch of lies and so the broad wanted to believe her so we had a little argument. So I just decided that I would put all of my troubles in one big boat and let it sink but I was found just before I died. And another thing Daddy that bothered me a lot was Lou Ann, and I knew just how much you love me and how it hurted to see me go but Daddy I felt the same thing all the way out here and I still think the same thing. Daddy you don't know just how much I really wanted to stay with you but something somewhere kept telling me to go back to your mother. Then I would say I know my father and mother both love me so I just hate to break peoples hearts so I said to myself I hope my Daddy please understand I still love him even though I was going to come back home. But, Daddy even mother raised all of your kids there is no reason for me to say I don't want to stay with you but Daddy I understand what it means to you to have had me stay with you Daddy.

Oh yes, Daddy, Mother said answer her letter, and Dad, forgive me for the thing that I did *but Daddy you just don't know just how much I bare* (emphasis added). I am not trying to say that mother is not trying to help me but Daddy that little old woman can't take too much more of this so Daddy would you please come out this year and try to help us get back on our feet again and I am talking about all of us when I came home and did the wrong thing look like the world stopped with me. So Daddy I am back at home now I have been here for about a week now and I have started to school.

But Daddy I still haven't gotten everything I need so Daddy could you please send me some money this week.

But the reason I hadn't wrote you when I first got here, Daddy I had a little something to see about and I was kind of shook up for a while I was accused of having been responsible for having some three girls knocked up and they were suppose to all be mine but Daddy I proved it wasn't my fault that they were pregnant because I hadn't touched but one and she helped me beat that by saying that it wasn't mine. Daddy I don't want you to think that is the only reason I wouldn't stay is because I wanted to come back and start that same old dope drag over . . . see Daddy just before I came out I had started to try and be a pimp and when I came back here I tried once more and I fail but not bad because I live on my name alone. So I decided to come home before I get in some kind of trouble up here and take or ruin my home up here but Daddy I just couldn't get used to your city.

P.S. Daddy do you really think Mt. Adams has more to offer than L.A.? L.A. IS WHERE I STAY. BYE FOR NOW. ANSWER SOON. LOVE, Ray

Daddy I tried as hard I could to make it cheerful but it does get sad. Daddy I am up by myself. I been up all night trying to write you something to cheer you up because I could see your heart breaking when you first asked Sam's wife if they would have room and that Sunday Dad it hard but I fought the tears that burned my eyes as we drove off and Daddy part of my sickness when I had taken an overdose I did just want to sleep myself away because I missed you Dad. You made me feel like I just found where I belong just like a lost piece of puzzle.

But when I left I felt like I had killed something inside of you and I knew you hated to see me go and I hated to go to but Daddy well I kind of missed mother and after all I had seen her I miss you and remembered what you said I settle down but Daddy I tried hard so I went and bought some sleeping pills and took so both of you could feel the same thing.

Long-standing History of Problems

A consideration of the long-standing nature of the adolescent's problems is a necessary prerequisite to understanding why the explanation of a suicide attempt in terms of "precipitating causes" is not sufficient. Such precipitating causes do not serve per se to precipitate the suicide attempt. It is only in the context of the adolescent's total biography that such events have any significance.

Granted, the long-standing problems may vary with social class, ethnicity, or family structure. No matter what form they take, their existence is seen in general to be a necessary condition for the suicide attempt. Many of the characteristics found in the suicide note above are common to a great majority of the case histories studied thus far, i.e. broken homes, problems developing from love affairs, rejection by parents, financial problems, rural to urban shifts, placement or threatened placement in foster homes or juvenile halls, and conflicts between parent and adolescent over behavioral problems (*see* Table 7-I) and disciplinary techniques.

It is important to bear in mind that these problems are numerous and serious and serve to progressively isolate the adolescent from meaningful social relationships (*see* Table 7-II). *This isolation, in turn, constitutes the problem and at the same time serves to isolate the adolescent from any possibility of solving it.*

TABLE 7-I

**Behavioral Problems Seen as Adaptive Techniques in
Adolescents Who Have Attempted Suicide**

Percent	Problems
	1) gloominess 2) won't talk 3) withdrawn
65	Exhibited one or more of these behavioral problems and believe them to have originated within the last five years.
21	Exhibited one or more of these behavioral problems "all my life."
14	Claim none of these behavioral problems.
	1) sassiness 2) defiance 3) rebelliousness
85	Exhibited one or more of these behavioral problems and believe them to have originated within the last five years.
28	Exhibited one or more of these behavioral problems "all my life."
14	Claim none of these behavioral problems.
70	Have run away from home one or more times in the last five years.
25	Have engaged in physical violence against parent(s) or other relatives and/or "temper tantrums" which began in the last few years.
86	Have "functional physical complaints not given to specific diagnosis."
50	Have illnesses which are clearly psychosomatic in nature.

TABLE 7-II

Long-Standing History of Problems Among
Adolescents Who Have Attempted Suicide

Percent	Description of Problem
88	Families have one or both natural parents missing.
31	Families consist of only one parent.
42	All adolescents had stepparents.
100	Adolescents with stepparents experienced a great many problems because of this situation. All stepparents were "unwanted" stepparents.
13	Adolescents lived with neither natural nor stepparents, i.e. lived in foster homes or with other relatives.
70	Parents had been married more than once.
37	Families experience alcoholism in mother or father as a serious problem.
65	Families have subjected the adolescent to an extreme number of environmental changes, (residential moves, school changes, family structure changes, etc.).
85	Adolescents view their total family conflict as extreme.
30	Families are in the "poverty" income category, i.e. $2700 or less annual income.

The Escalation Stage

Following a long-standing history of problems, there is an intermediate stage characterized by an escalation of problems within the last five years.

In our society adolescence is a particularly stressful time of life for the teenager and his parents. An inquiry into the conflict stemming from adolescent behavioral problems and parental disciplinary techniques designed to cope with them reveals an interesting aspect of the escalation stage within the family setting.

The paucity of solutions to these problems does not usually stem from any initial lack of effort by the adolescent and/or parent to resolve them. Paradoxically, the greater the parental effort to resolve the total family conflict stemming from adolescent behavioral problems, the greater was the resulting family conflict. The dynamics of this seeming paradox is made understandable within the following conceptual framework.

Preliminary findings indicate that 69 percent of all behavioral problems that the adolescent suicide attempter reports he has engaged in (according to his own account) began within the past five years. Other than the suicide attempt, there are essentially five ways in which the adolescent can attempt to cope with his problems: physical aggression, rebellion, withdrawal (a distinct lack of affect), physical separation from the problem (going to one's room or running away from home), or internalization of the problem where it manifests itself in the form of psychosomatic illness (*see* Table 7-I).

When a high percentage of the total family conflict, which has escalated within the last year or two to an intolerable level, is a result of the parents' attempt to resolve their adolescent's behavioral problems, it is not surprising that their efforts have proven eminently unsuccessful. Whereas the average percent of difference in perception between the adolescent and the parent with respect to the average number of his behavioral problems is only two percent, i.e. the parent and adolescent both feel that the adolescent has an average of eight behavioral problems, the average percent of difference in perception between the adolescent and the parent with respect to which behavioral problems the adolescent engages in is 35 percent.

The implications of these findings are clear. The adolescent feels that approximately one-third of the behavioral problems that the parent attributes to him do not exist. By the same token, he may feel that the parent is either unaware of or indifferent to approximately one-third of the behavioral problems he does have. Any initial optimism that the parent or teenager might entertain by way of converting the other to a position of right thinking, will decrease at about the same rate that the frustration level increases. The result is a double bind.

On the one hand, the parents' efforts at reforming the adolescent often seem inappropriate to the adolescent and are considered nagging, the form of discipline our study thus far reveals to be most noxious to the adolescent. On the other hand, the parents' failure to influence the adolescent to cease in behavior that the adolescent feels is bad, and which he could and would gladly forego with parental aid, is taken by him as a sign of rejection.

The net result from the perspective of the parent is getting nowhere in a hurry and increased frustration, which in turn leads to the vicious cycle of trying to reduce the dilemma by trying harder. This appears to the adolescent in the form of either increased nagging and rejection or the inappropriate use by the parents of even more severe disciplinary procedures, e.g. withholding privileges. (*Withholding privileges* is the discipline *most often* used by the parent for the *most serious* problems.)

 Both the parent and the adolescent, once captives of this squirrel-cage predicament, are likely to fail in their efforts to resolve their differences and to reduce the total family conflict to a tolerable level. The above conditions lead to a worsening of the relationship until it is eclipsed in a mutual feeling of frustration, which in turn leads to an uneasy resignation, and both stop trying. This is accompanied by the usual cessation of communication, verbal and otherwise, i.e. lack of affect, going to one's room, running away from home, and seeking to confide in persons other than parents.

This process is important not only in helping to explain part of the high level of conflict within the families of adolescents who attempt suicide, but serves the further purpose of providing a perspective for the more general problem of intergenerational differences. The above account does not explain the very important question of how these differences in perception arose in the first place or how they were maintained over time, notwithstanding the initial conscious efforts of both parties to resolve them.

What is at least partially responsible for the reluctance of the adolescent and parents to give up is the presumption on the part of both that they are rational. "You can tell me; I'll understand,"

"I was young once too," or for the adolescent, "I'm older than you think," are all expressions that indicate not only a willingness to listen but imply a reciprocal ability to understand and empathize. To deny the existence of this condition would be to admit that the parent and adolescent were incapable of understanding each other and that all attempts at a meaningful exchange of ideas and any possible resolution of problems by way of this would be futile. Thus far, all the adolescents who have attempted suicide have characterized the relationship with their parents as a breakdown in communication and as a general feeling of "If they don't care, I don't either."

It is not only in the area of behavioral problems that this process works to escalate the total family conflict suddenly and inexplicably. Disciplinary techniques, the counterbalance to behavioral problems, works in the same way to aggravate matters. The average percent of difference in perception between the adolescent and parent with regard to the *number* and *kind* of disciplines used by the parent is 2.2 percent and 34 percent, respectively. The implications of this statistic and how this difference in perception works to escalate conflict for the adolescent and parent are discussed previously under behavioral problems. This topic will receive further consideration in Chapter 9.

While nonsuicidal adolescents and their parents also experience this escalation phenomenon to an extent, they are not asked to contend simultaneously with a biography of problems of the same order as those experienced by suicidal adolescents in our study. A precipitating cause or set of causes described in the dynamics of the final period must be viewed in the context of the total biography to render it meaningful. Otherwise people may appear to others to be attempting suicide over the most trivial incidents, which encourages the latter to label the former *irrational, impulsive,* or *mentally ill.*

The Final Stage

Failing a resolution of the problems described in the first two stages, the adolescent enters the final phase characterized by the no-chance attitude. In general, the final stage finds the adolescent experiencing a chain-reaction dissolution of any remaining meaningful social relationships. Already alienated from his parents, the adolescent may seek the closeness of a primary relationship in a romance. His relations with peers and the school often undergo changes as well.

The Romance

Three-fourths of our sample thus far is comprised of females and about 30 percent of these, or about one-fourth of all cases, are pregnant. A romance — sometimes resulting in a pregnancy — may well culminate in a suicide attempt if left to run its course without corrective intervention.

The adolescent, already alienated to a great extent from the parents, seeks love, understanding, acceptance, reason, predictability — in short, a meaningful social relationship in one of the few remaining forms that allows for the intimacy implicit in such a relationship, i.e. a boyfriend or girlfriend. In pursuing this, the adolescent alienates most of his remaining friends and associates by spending all of his time on the romance. Parents who are against the adolescent's forming a serious attachment at such an early age disapprove of these new behaviors, e.g. staying out late, wanting to go out more often, or demanding greater autonomy.

When the love affair culminates in a pregnancy the problems are compounded and often result in a rapid disintegration of social relationships on all fronts. The boyfriend disappears, other friends have already been alienated, and the parents are completely disillusioned and give up at the very time help is most needed. Nasty rumors circulate at school among her peers, she is no longer participating in sports or other school activities, and her school work usually suffers.

To illustrate the level of desperation that a pregnant adolescent may experience and the lengths to which she will go to secure meaningful social relationships (and at the same time attempt to solve the problem of pregnancy) consider the following letter a teenager wrote the night of the suicide attempt to her boyfriend:

Dear Bill,

I want you and I to get an understanding about certain things because I think you got the wrong impression on me. I have the feeling that you think I been doing immoral things with elder men. But I glad you think that. It makes me feel that my plan is working. I rather for people to think that then know the truth. But I want you to know the truth. The real reason why I staying too late, getting into mischief is I want to get sent to Juvy (juvenile hall) for about eight months. Bill you know I deliberately lied to you about my age. I know you would find out sooner or later and you did. But I thought maybe you wouldn't care. I thought that you could learn to like me, just a little. But I notice many times that I was wrong by your reaction. But I still couldn't give you up. I didn't want to admit the truth. I thought I still had a chance to succeed. But instead I found myself practicing methods to get you. But I chicken out to try. *I found myself needing you, living to be with you* (emphasis added). Know all the time I was making a fool out of myself. But I didn't care. I needed you more than anything in the world. But all the time I knew deep inside behind the close door there was something but in the open there was nothing. And believe me it hurt. I knew all the time you were hinting to me I was too young, didn't know nothing about life. But you were wrong. I know a whole lot about life. I'm ashamed of the things I know to be so young. I couldn't face, of what you might have said. And I sure it would have hurt my feelings badly. I'm two months pregnant by you. You don't have to admit it. I don't care. You may say anything you like. You don't have to worry about any trouble, it would be a disgrace for me to let people know I threw myself on you knowing that you didn't care or feel anyway toward me. Don't worry no one will ever know my childs father. I never mention you to him or her which ever it be.   J.A.

Other Considerations

About one-third of the adolescents who attempted suicide were not enrolled in school at the time of the attempt. Yet, none of these adolescents had dropped out because of poor scholarship.

Reasons for nonattendance in school were almost always events that contributed to the suicide attempt itself: prior suicide attempts, pregnancy, behavioral problems, or institutionalization (in the hospital or juvenile hall). Adolescents not attending school are excluded from one of the most important resources for establishing and maintaining meaningful social relationships.

Another link in the chain-reaction dissolution of meaningful social relationships is often the loss of an older sibling from the household. Thus far it appears that whether families are large or small, they are characterized by an exodus of brothers and sisters at the earliest possible moment. They marry, join the Army, and move in with friends or other relatives. This systematic exodus leads to a reordering of the family structure and constitutes another problem faced by the adolescent, especially since the sibling often represents one of the few remaining meaningful social relationships. Although this exodus of siblings often occurs in the final stage of the process, it may also be characteristic of one of the earlier stages, usually the escalation period. By the end of the final stage a "suicide attempt" (where death is not intended) occurs to the adolescent in a last desperate effort to find some means of resolving his problems by bringing them to the attention of his parents and significant others.

Rather than reducing the total problem faced by the adolescent, the "suicide attempt" itself becomes a problem and serves only to add to the alienation, rumors, etc. that he is already forced to contend with. It is the presumption of the parents and peers that anyone attempting suicide is cowardly, mentally ill, or has something horrible or shameful to hide. For those who had a history of previous attempts (63 percent), these attempts followed in close sequence. This is not surprising since the suicide attempt itself often serves to increase rather than decrease the problems that the adolescent faces. Shneidman has noted that "physicians and relatives must be especially cautious and watchful for at least 90 days after a person who has been suicidal appears to be improving."[5]

One might expect that anyone experiencing a long-standing history of problems and a more recent period of escalation of these and new problems, most of which are not given to any solution known to the individual and which culminate in a situation of social isolation, would come to consider death (suicide) as the only solution to the problem of living. It is interesting to note that the adolescents in this study who experienced the kinds of problems and social relations characterized in this paper did not experience these things in a vacuum, but as a member of a family and a group of friends with things in common. Relatives and friends who experienced similar conditions and comparable life chances often arrived at the same view at some previous time — that suicide is the only way out.

In 44 percent of all cases there has been a successful suicide or suicide attempt by one or more close friends or relatives; and in 25 percent of all cases there has been a suicide attempt by the mother or father of the adolescent. A suicide attempt by a parent or significant other serves to lessen for the adolescent the social constraints against suicide. Indeed, a parent's suicide attempt tends to legitimate the adolescent's attempt or proposed attempt: "If they can, I can too."

It also serves as a model and offers a possible solution to one's problems, a solution the parent attempted. In this case the parent is seen as *the model* on which the adolescent is expected to pattern his behavior. Information received from the parents indicates that they have experienced many of the same problems that their adolescents have.

The mothers of all males who attempted suicide had either had illegitimate children or were forced into marriages because of pregnancy. Twenty-seven percent of all mothers interviewed had either illegitimate children or forced marriages because of pregnancy. Seventy percent of the mothers were separated or divorced. Thirty-eight percent had married more than once, and many of these marriages of convenience proved to be short-lived. A very high percentage of all parents had also suffered economic deprivation. In brief, persons who are subject to the constraints of a similar set of life chances are likely, in many basic regards, to end with similar biographies.

Summary

Precipitating causes can only be meaningfully evaluated within the context of the individual's total biography and from the perspective of what these situations have meant to him. The process whereby the adolescent comes to view suicide as the only solution is seen to result from a progression of his problems through three stages: (1) a long-standing history of problems, (2) a period of escalation of problems above and beyond those usually associated with adolescence, and (3) a final stage, a recent onslaught of problems usually characterized by a chain-reaction dissolution of any remaining meaningful social relationships. This progressive social isolation constitutes the problem and at the same time serves to prevent the adolescent from securing any possible means of resolving it.

REFERENCES

1. Dublin, L.: *Suicide.* New York, Ronald Press, 1963.
2. Farberow, N., Shneidman, E., and Litman, R.E.: The suicidal patient and the physician. *Mind, 1*:69-75, 1963.
3. Jacobziner, H.: Attempted suicides in adolescence. *J.A.M.A., 191*:101-105, 1965.
4. Schuetz, A.: *Collected Papers. Vol. I.: The Problem of Social Reality.* The Hague, Martinus Nijhoff, 1962.
5. Shneidman, E., and Farberow, N.: Clues to suicide. In Shneidman, E., and Farberow, N. (Eds.): *Clues to Suicide.* New York, McGraw-Hill Paperbacks, 1957.
6. Thomas, W.I., and Znaniecki, F.: *The Polish Peasant in Europe and America,* Vol II. Boston, Gorham Press, 1927.
7. Wahl, C.W.: Suicide as a magical act. In Shneidman, E., and Farberow, N. (Eds.): *Clues to Suicide.* New York, McGraw-Hill Paperbacks, 1957.

Chapter 8

BROKEN HOMES AND
SOCIAL ISOLATION IN ATTEMPTED
SUICIDES OF ADOLESCENTS

THIS paper deals with an analysis of a key concept in the psychiatric literature on suicide: broken homes. By comparing the life histories of fifty adolescent suicide attempters with those of thirty-two control adolescents, we sought to better understand the process whereby *broken homes* and the implicit *loss of a love object* worked to progressively isolate the adolescent from meaningful social relationships. It is this latter condition that we feel ultimately led the adolescent to attempt suicide.

The Problem

The authors wish to begin by acknowledging their debt to Durkheim. The notion of certain social structural events, serving to isolate the individual from meaningful social relationships and leading to a lack of social integration, is central to the formulation to be presented in this paper. However, Durkheim's success in *Suicide,*[8] in discrediting psychological explanations and legitimizing sociological explanations of suicide, rested more upon his eloquence than the strength of his argument. The etiological approach as a model methodology for the study of suicide has only recently come under serious attack.[7, 16] The authors feel that Durkheim was premature in abandoning the morphological approach and the use of case history materials and suicide notes as a source of data. The basis of this rejection rested largely upon his contention that one was unlikely to find a common denominator in the life situations of suicides. This belief was founded upon the observation that the range of personal circumstances immediately preceding the suicide, usually referred to now as *precipitating causes,* were almost infinite in number. For example, we are told: "... some men resist horrible misfortune, while others kill themselves after slight troubles," or that "... those who suffer most are not those who kill themselves most."[9] Thus, Durkheim held little hope of classifying different types of suicides on the basis of the victim's particular life situation. It is noteworthy, of course, that he had never actually undertaken such a study but had abandoned the search for a common denominator before having begun it. The authors believe that the above common-sense assumptions are unwarranted. Indeed, if one need intuit, as Durkheim has done, the effects of one's personal situation on suicide, we feel the intuition of Hume is much more consistent with our findings on suicidal adolescents:

> I believe that no man ever threw away life, while it was worth keeping. For such is our natural horror of death, that small motives will never be able to reconcile us to it; and though perhaps the situation of a man's health or fortune did not seem to require this remedy, we may at least be assured, that anyone who, without apparent reason, has had recourse to it, was curst with such an incurable depravity or gloominess of temper as must poison all enjoyment, and render him equally miserable as if he had been loaded with the most grievous misfortunes.[11]

In concluding his argument on the futility of attempting to classify suicides according to morphological types, Durkheim states, "Accordingly, even those who have ascribed most influence to individual conditions have sought these conditions less in such external incidents than in the intrinsic nature of the person, that is, his biological constitution and the physical concomitants on which it depends."[10] This has been the general approach of psychiatrists, psychologists, and some less positivistic sociologists. Such a perspective has led Shneidman and Farberow[17] and Tuckman et al.[22] to view suicide notes as lending themselves to projective techniques where the contents of the notes are seen to be indicative of the real, underlying, deeper truth of what is really going on: "They (suicide notes) strongly suggest the possibility of viewing them as projective devices (in much the same way as MAPS tests of TAT protocols are projective products) from which information may be *inferred* about the subject" (emphasis added).[18]

In their search for hidden motives to be inferred from the notes, Tuckman et al. are struck by the suicides' apparent rationality. "In this study the writers were impressed with the possibility that in a number of cases the suicide could have resulted from a conscious, 'rational' decision reached by weighing the pros and cons of continuing to live, although to a lesser extent unconscious factors *may* have been operating" (emphasis added).[23] The conscious, rational elements are striking. The unconscious, irrational factors to a lesser extent *may* have been operating.

It is from the latter, deeper, biological perspective that psychiatrists tend to interpret the accounts of their patients, the apparent rational aspects notwithstanding: "The view to be presented in this paper is that suicide is not pre-eminently a rational act pursued to achieve rational ends, even when it is effected by persons who appear to be eminently rational. Rather, it is a magical act, actuated to achieve irrational, delusional, and illusory ends."[25]

The case against irrational suicide is made by Tuckman et al. as well. They note that particularly in the older age groups, "The wish for relief from dissatisfying life experiences becomes so strong that thoughts are not of self-destruction but of relief from extreme discomfort."[24] In this study the authors feel that the dissatisfying life experiences among the adolescent suicide attempters also led them to consider and attempt suicide. Their life histories as related by them and their parents lend support to the proposition that suicide attempts among adolescents follow a conscious deliberation of the pros and cons of living, where the final decision rests ultimately upon the sequential ordering of real life events in the biography of the suicidal persons and whether or not these events led to his progressive isolation from all meaningful social relationships.

Kahne, in reviewing the medical literature, has noted the paucity of studies dealing with the life situations of suicides.[12] Sociology, too, has tended to ignore life histories and has followed Durkheim's recommendation on the assumption that an explanation of suicide rates is best achieved through the etiological approach (an approach that Durkheim used to discredit psychological explanations and establish sociological ones). On the other hand, psychiatrists and psychologists have used the morphological approach based on the intrinsic nature of the person, that is his biological constitution and the physical concomitants on which it depends. Here it is presumed that if the etiological approach based on social facts is best for explaining official suicide rates, morphological procedures based on psychological and psychiatric assumptions are best for explaining the essential characteristics of suicide.

The approach used by the authors can be described as a synthesis of certain aspects of both of the above systems, i.e. a morphological approach emphasizing the social-structural aspects of adolescent suicide attempters (and a control group of nonattempters), considered within the context of their life histories. Unlike Durkheim, we believe there are aspects of life situations common to all and that independent of any particular content (problems or means of coping), the life situation of adolescents attempting suicide adheres in its formal features to a process, one to which the control adolescents, matched on age, race, sex, and net family income were not subject. Having described the sample of adolescents in the preceeding chapter, we will go on to a more detailed description of the methodology and its relationship to the study of broken homes and suicide.

Method

Each adolescent in the experimental group was interviewed within twenty-four to fourty-eight hours of the actual suicide attempt by the sociologist or his research assistant and the psychiatrist. As previously noted in Chapter 7, a structured interview schedule was used covering the following areas: (1) the suicide attempt, (2) family relations, (3) peer relations, (4) attitudes toward and performance in school, and (5) career aspirations. The attempter's parent was also interviewed, using a structured interview schedule that covered the same areas but with an additional section on the adolescent's developmental history. Each interview required between one and two hours to complete.

Both adolescent and parent completed identical questionnaires covering behavioral problems and disciplinary techniques, which provided essentially two separate versions of these situations. The teenagers in the control group and their parents received the same interviews as the experimental group, minus the section on the suicide attempt itself. They also completed the questionnaires on behavioral problems and disciplinary techniques.

Therapy was offered to each suicide attempter, and the sessions of those accepting were recorded. The taped therapy sessions were then transcribed.

The data received from the interviews was put into case history form according to a standard format based on the five areas mentioned above. An attempt was made to thus place the data in the context of the adolescent's total biography where particular attention could then be directed not only to the events, but, more significantly, to their sequential ordering. This data took the form, essentially, of two stories: the parent's biography of the adolescent and the adolescent's autobiography. The two comprised a single case history. Additionally, information obtained from an analysis of transcriptions made of taped therapy sessions of thirty of the fifty adolescents, suicide notes written by the attempter to parents or boyfriends, and letters or outside information received from others after the fact were also incorporated into the case histories when available.

On the basis of these case histories, incorporating the above sources of data, a life history chart was constructed for each experimental and control adolescent. This was done by putting all of the events recorded in the case history into chronological order along a vertical continuum depicting graphically the experiences of the adolescent from birth until the time of the last suicide attempt (43 percent had more than one attempt). In addition, whatever sparse background information was obtained on the parent interviewed was also included in the life history chart. The charts took the form shown in Figure 8-1.

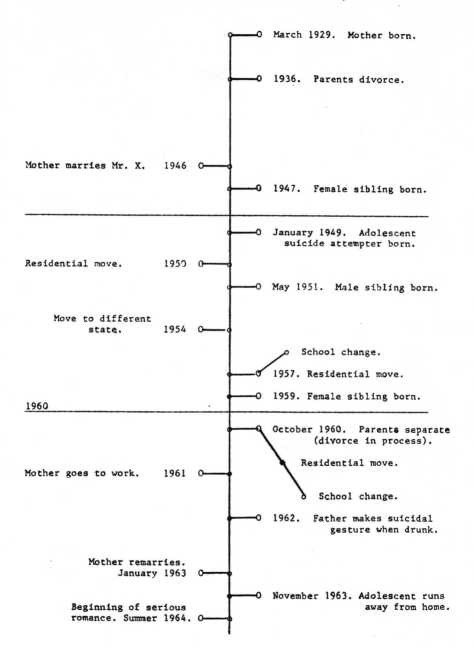

Figure 8-1

The charts depict graphically and in considerable detail the life histories of both the experimental and control adolescents. The dots appear in different colors and markings representing nineteen categories of events, for example residential moves, school changes, onset of various behavioral problems, separation or divorce of parents, acquisition of a stepparent, suicide attempts, deaths in family, etc.

By comparing the distribution of the colored dots and the comments accompanying them for the experimental and control groups, we can see not only what was experienced by the two sets of adolescents, but more significantly, what the sequential ordering of these events were and how they tended to pile up or not, depending on their chronology. This allows us to view the precipitating event not as a particular isolated crisis, but within the context of the adolescent's total biography. From this perspective the adolescent no longer seems to be attempting suicide over some trivial isolated problem. The findings also seriously call into question the notion that adolescent suicide attempts are essentially unconscious, irrational, or impulsive in nature.

An Analysis of the Data and Discussion of the Findings

In seeking a common denominator in the life histories of adolescent suicide attempters that distinguishes them from the control adolescents, the factors sought were not isolated or independent events. What we were attempting to delineate were the formal aspects of a process through which the adolescent had to progress in order to, first, entertain, and then, attempt suicide. The general approach of the authors was social-psychological. We felt it was necessary to consider two basic aspects in describing such a process: (1) the formal aspects of the sequential ordering of the external events in the everyday life of the adolescent and (2) how the adolescent experienced these events and reacted to them.

The necessity for an evaluation of the second step is based on a key assumption of psychiatry and psychology — that two persons subject to the same event can experience it differently and that one's behavior is based ultimately upon the experience and not the event. There stems from this contention the necessity of allowing for personal differences. Granted, there is a range of occurrences in which the same event may be viewed and experienced differently by different persons. It is also true that there are many events that persons in like situations seem to view and experience in the same way. Indeed, it is on the continuation of this process that society is based. For example, 40 percent of the adolescent suicide attempters had stepparents, usually stepfathers, and in every case this stepparent was seen as unwanted. The alienation of parents, broken romances, pregnancies, etc., were without exception viewed as unwelcome events. Keeping in mind that there is no natural necessity involved in the above consensus, i.e. the adolescent might love his stepparent, feel he is well rid of a sweetheart, or welcome the birth of a child, it was nevertheless true that with respect to the adolescents studied, this was not the case.

Making allowances for individual differences to provide the exception, the rule seems to be, with respect to those events listed above and others to be considered at a later date, all are experienced as unwelcomed and result in the adolescent's unhappiness. If a series of these events occur in the particular sequence outlined in the three-stage process given in Chapter 7, they seem to result in the adolescent's experiencing extreme unhappiness and withdrawal. Why should this be? It is postulated that these events (or comparable ones) experienced by the adolescent in the right sequence will lead to his progressive unhappiness because they have led to his progressive isolation from meaningful social relationships. This isolation, in turn, is seen by the adolescent as the problem and simultaneously serves to isolate him from gaining access to that segment of the population necessary to resolve the problem, i.e. helping him to reestablish a meaningful social relationship.

Keeping in mind that certain events may be experienced in the same way and that these result in the adolescent's progressive unhappiness, a state he projects into a pessimistic future world view, the central concern of this paper will be to compare the presence or absence and sequential ordering of these events in the life histories of fifty adolescent suicide attempters and thirty-two control adolescents matched on age, race, sex, and net family income.

It seems a distinct advantage to view events in a chronological order in an attempt to find a common denominator in some series of events that progress toward a common end — isolation from meaningful social relationships — which is responsible for the suicide attempt. From this perspective, any particular variable (broken homes) or set of variables should be viewed not in isolation but rather with respect to when it occurs, and perhaps reoccurs, within the context of the adolescent's biography. It is only in this way that any particular event can take on the meaning that one associates with a significant event.

The advantage of the above perspective can be demonstrated best where it is presumed least. For example, the life histories of 72 percent of the suicide attempters and 53 percent of the control adolescents indicated broken homes. There is a considerable literature on the effects of broken homes on suicide and suicide attempts.

Dorpat et al., in a review of the psychiatric literature, report that estimates of broken homes among suicide attempters range from 38 percent to 84 percent.[3] Significantly, it is noted that, "All of the groups of attempted suicides studied were highly selected groups and *no data for control groups were given*" (emphasis added).[4] Their own study comparing rates of broken homes among 114 completed suicides and 121 suicide attempters found 63 percent of the suicide attempters and 50 percent of the suicides had broken homes. Again, no attempt was made to evaluate the chronology of events: "Where several types of loss occurred for a single subject, categorization was based on the type of loss which occurred first."[5]

Our own data indicate that the control adolescents, matched on age, race, sex and net family income, have a rate of broken homes in excess of the lowest estimate for suicide attempters cited by Dorpat.[21] Then, too, why did 72 percent of the experimental adolescents with broken homes attempt suicide when 53 percent of the control adolescents with broken homes did not?

The answer will not be found in the significant correlation of some unidimensional explanation, i.e. broken homes, where the event is viewed ahistorically. An analysis that placed broken homes into the context of the adolescent's complete biography, so that its effects on the adolescent were better understood, proved helpful in resolving the above dilemma. From this perspective, the contradiction proved more apparent than real. For example, although 72 percent of the suicide attempters and 53 percent of the control adolescents experienced broken homes (most of which occurred at an early age), 58 percent of the suicide attempters' parents remarried while only 25 percent of the control adolescents' parents did so. Further, the control parents who did remarry did so early in the adolescent's life and remained married. The parents of suicide attempters either remarried later in the adolescent's life or if they remarried early were divorced and remarried several more times. The result of this chronology is that 56 percent of the suicide attempters' parents and only 10 percent of the control adolescents' parents were divorced, separated, or remarried within the past five years, i.e. since the onset of adolescence. The effects of this upon the adolescent should be clear. Whereas both the experimental and control groups of adolescents experienced a high percentage of broken homes, the control group had experienced a stable home life during the last five years while the suicide attempters had not. This is particularly significant, not only because divorce, separation, or the acquisition of a stepparent is a stressful and disruptive event per se, but also because it occurs during a particularly stressful time in the life cycle — adolescence.

Dorpat et al. contend that their findings lend support to the theories of Bowlby and Zilboorg, ". . .that parental loss in childhood predisposes to depression and suicide later in life."[6] Our own findings do not tend to support this. Both the suicide attempters and control adolescents had high rates of parental loss in childhood. One group attempted suicide; the other did not.

What of the second aspect, the relationship between childhood parental loss and depression in later life? This, too, is not supported by our findings. Whereas both the experimental and control groups of adolescents experienced high rates of parental loss in childhood, nearly twice as many suicide attempters experienced the onset of symptoms of depression (gloominess, won't talk, or withdrawal) later in life (within the last five years) as did the control adolescents. Eighty percent of the suicide attempters experienced one or more symptoms of depression while only 45 percent of the control adolescents had this experience.

Therefore, it is not parental loss in childhood per se that predisposes to depression and suicides in later life. Loss of love object is an important aspect of the process, but it must be viewed as part of a process where particular attention is paid to when it occurred and/or reoccurred, and not merely to its presence or absence. Furthermore, it seems that it is not the loss of a love object per se that is so distressing but the loss of love, i.e. the reciprocal intimacy, spontaneity, and closeness that one experiences in a primary relationship.

Regarding the loss of a love object, another aspect to be considered is whether or not the object need be physically absent to be lost. That is, in broken or nonbroken homes, where one or both natural parents may be present, might not the adolescent still experience loss of a love object? We believe he can. Both from the interviews and from the questionnaire data, it is clear that the suicide attempter was alienated from his parents more frequently, and to a greater degree, than the control adolescent, especially during the escalation stage.

TABLE 8-I

		Agree or Strongly Agree		
	Experimental Male %	Control Male %	Experimental Female %	Control Female %
1. I agree with my parents about what things are important in life.	45	66	58	86
2. It's hard for me to talk to my parents about my problems because they argue.	45	11	44	14
3. When you tell your parents the truth they sometimes punish you.	63	45	72	19
4. When you talk to your parents it's best to be careful what you say.	72	33	49	32
5. I really don't know how to talk to my parents.	54	0	55	28
6. No matter what my problem might be I know my parents will stand behind me.	36	55	46	80
7. If I had a choice I would prefer stepparents to my natural parents.	18	0	7	0

Only five suicide attempters (four of whom had never had a stepparent) and none of the control adolescents preferred step-parents to their natural parents. This takes on significance when one considers that 40 percent (twenty) of the suicide attempters and only 16 percent (five) of the control adolescents had a step-parent at some time in their lives.

Following the alienation between the parents and the suicide attempter, the adolescent seeks to reestablish a meaningful social relationship in one of the few remaining situations that allow for it — a romance with a boyfriend or girlfriend. During this courtship, often described as *possessive,* the adolescent alienates casual friends by concentrating all of his time and energy in establishing within the romance the relationship he seeks. When the romance fails, there results a feeling that Kobler and Stotland[13] refer to as the end of hope.

It is significant that whereas 38 percent (nineteen) of the suicide attempters and 23 percent (seven) of the control adolescents were involved in a serious romance, 58 percent of the suicide attempters' romances (eleven) and 0 percent of the control adolescents' romances were in the terminal stages at the time of the interviews. Further, five of the fourteen experimental females and none of the control females involved in a serious romance were either pregnant or feared themselves pregnant as a result of the romance. The pregnancy led inevitably to a total withdrawal and rejection by the boyfriend, and usually by the parents, at a time when acceptance was most needed.

The state of depression characteristic of adolescents who attempt suicide stems from a series of real life experiences. Although most people accept as a truism that we all have our ups and downs, the perspective of the suicide attempter at the time of his interview was that his life was not characterized by ups and downs, but only downs. We feel it is unwarranted to attribute this belief to a restricted view of reality stemming from a state of depression. By comparing the life histories of the experimental and control adolescents, there is good evidence to show that this weltanschauung is justified by the suicide attempters' real life experiences. Thirty-eight percent of the suicide attempters and 94 percent of the control adolescents considered their childhoods to have been happy ones. Again, judging from the events in their life histories, the discrepancy between these two statistics seems to the authors to be based on a firm recognition of reality. Indeed, it would appear that only a distortion or denial of reality by the suicide attempter would have been helpful in forestalling the attempt.

Conclusions

The authors have attempted to demonstrate the use of the case history approach for the study of adolescent suicide attempts. Particular effort was made to overcome Durkheim's criticisms of this method, noted earlier, by seeking the common denominator in the personal situations of suicidal persons in a process, rather than in some independent event. We also feel that the procedure outlined in this paper overcomes the telling criticisms of C. Wright Mills of those who infer prior biological causes or motives from the verbalizations of the actor.

The question arises: What of those persons who have experienced a series of problems in the sequence described in the three-stage process where the problems led to their progressive isolation from meaningful social relationships, but who did not attempt suicide? The authors can only state that no such exceptions were found in the life histories of the adolescent suicide attempters we have studied or in other thorough case studies of suicidal persons in the literature.[1, 2, 14, 19]

Judging from the verbatim accounts of the suicide attempters in the interviews as well as in suicide notes left by them (and notes written by other adolescents outside our sample), the decision to suicide was the result of a rational decision-making process. However, the choice of death is not based on a desire to die. They would, if they could, choose to live. Death in a sense is not chosen at all, but results from the progressive failure of adaptive techniques to cope with the problems of living, where *the* problem is the maintenance of meaningful social relationships. In short, the potential suicide felt that he had no choice, i.e. death is necessary. It is from this recognition of necessity that his sense of freedom stems, and immediately preceding the act itself there is often a feeling of well-being, a cessation of all cares. This is evidenced in the matter-of-fact presentation found in suicide notes.

The relationship of broken homes and loss of a love object to suicide and suicide attempts has been an issue of central concern in the psychiatric literature. The authors feel that the significance of these concepts is better explained as a continuing process to which the individual is subject, rather than some unique traumatic event of early childhood which in and of itself predisposes the individual to depression and suicidal tendencies in later life. Without this perspective there is no way of explaining why the control adolescents who also experienced a parental loss in early childhood were not disposed to suicide in later life and were far less disposed to symptoms of depression. In light of this, we feel that the authors' explanation goes further than the traditional psychiatric explanations in explaining how broken homes and loss of love object result in establishing suicidal tendencies in an individual.

REFERENCES

1. Binswanger, Ludwig: The case of Ellen West. In May, Rollo, et al. (Eds.): *Existence.* New York, Basic Books, 1958.
2. Cavan, Ruth S.: *Suicide,* Case XXIX, Marian Blake and her loves, and Case XXX, A youth who was prematurely tired. Chicago, University of Chicago Press, 1928, pp. 198-245.
3. Dorpat, Theodore L., et al.: Broken homes and attempted and completed suicide. *Archives of General Psychiatry, 12:*213, February 1965.
4. Ibid.
5. Ibid.
6. Dorpat, op. cit., p. 216.
7. Douglas, Jack D.: *The Sociological Study of Suicide: Suicidal Actions as Socially Meaningful Actions.* In press, Princeton University Press.
8. Durkheim, Emile: *Suicide: A Study in Sociology.* New York, The Free Press, 1951, p. 298.
9. Durkheim, op. cit., p. 298.
10. Ibid.
11. Hume, David: Of suicide. In MacIntyre, Alasdair (Ed.): *Hume's Ethical Writings.* New York, Collier Books, 1965, p. 305.
12. Kahne, Merton J.: Suicide research: A critical review of strategies and potentialities in Mental Hospitals. *The International Journal of Social Psychiatry, 12*(2):120-129, Spring, 1966.
13. Kobler, A.L., and Stotland, Ezra: *The End of Hope.* New York, The Free Press, 1964.

14. Kobler and Stotland, op. cit.
15. Sacks, Harvey: Sociological description. *Berkeley Journal of Sociology,* *8*:1-16, 1963.
16. Shneidman, Edwin S., and Farberow, Norman L.: Appendix: Genuine and simulated suicide notes. In Shneidman, Edwin S., and Farberow, Norman L. (Eds.): *Clues to Suicide.* New York, McGraw-Hill, 1957.
17. Shneidman and Farberow, op. cit., 197.
18. Stengel, E., and Cook, Nancy: *Attempted Suicide: Its Social Significance and Effects.* New York, Oxford University Press, 1958.
19. Teicher, Joseph D., and Jacobs, Jerry: Adolescents who attempt suicide: Preliminary findings. *The American Journal of Psychiatry, 122*(11): 1248-1257, 1966.
20. Teicher, Joseph D., and Jacobs, Jerry: Adolescent suicide attempts: The culmination of a progressive social isolation. A paper read at the Annual Meeting of the American Orthopsychiatric Association, May, 1966.
21. Tuckman, Jacob, et al.: Emotional content of suicide notes. *The American Journal of Psychiatry, 116*(1):59-63, July, 1959.
22. Tuckman et al., op. cit., p. 62.
23. Ibid.
24. Wahl, Charles W.: Suicide as a magical act. In Shneidman, Edwin S., and Farberow, Norman L. (Eds.): *Clues to Suicide.* New York, McGraw-Hill, 1957.

Chapter 9

THE PHYSICIAN AND THE
ADOLESCENT SUICIDE ATTEMPTER

THE author's study of adolescent suicide attempters indicates
that the physician is in a unique and strategic social position
with respect to the potentially suicidal adolescent. The suicidal
patients studied were compared with a matched control group.
A total of 46 percent of the adolescent patients seen by the staff
of this study reported some contact with a doctor for some physical or mental complaint within the last year. In such cases the
doctor not only treated his patient for a specific complaint, but
also provided, from the adolescent's perspective, what may well be
the last and only possible resource for the resolution of his problem.

The statistics resulting from this study, as well as those of
other studies, are helpful insofar as they tend to indicate the extent to which the sequential ordering of events in the lives of
adolescent suicide attempters adhere to a particular pattern.
These and the biographies of the adolescent suicide attempters
(characterized by a three-stage progression to social isolation
which result in a suicide attempt) have been noted in preceding
chapters. The following provides some additional data, as it relates
to disciplinary techniques (used within the family), school, peers,
romances, and the role of all of these factors in contributing to
the adolescent's progressive social isolation from meaningful
social relationships. Given this isolation, the physician comes to
play a crucial role. How and why this is so will be dealt with later
in this chapter.

Discipline and the Family

The reciprocal effects of the disciplinary process on the adolescent and the parent of the experimental group are illuminating. We have seen in Chapter 7 how, on the one hand, the parents' efforts at reforming the adolescent often seem inappropriate and are considered to be nagging, a form of discipline that our study reveals is frequently used, especially by the mother. On the other hand, the parents' failure to discourage behaviors that the adolescent feels are bad and that he would gladly forego with parental aid is taken by him as a sign of rejection. The net results, from the perspective of the suicide attempter, is constant and inappropriate nagging, i.e. unfair discipline and/or rejection. The results from the perspective of the parent, is getting nowhere in a hurry and increased frustration, which in turn leads to the vicious cycle of trying to reduce the dilemma by trying harder. This appears to the adolescent in the form of either increased nagging and rejection or the inappropriate use by the parent of even more severe disciplinary procedures, e.g. withholding privileges is substituted for nagging or criticizing (*see* Table 9-I and 9-II).

The parents of suicide attempters who recently began to exhibit many new behavioral problems, believing that the adolescent would get into less trouble if he is watched more closely, frequently question him about his activities and whereabouts. This does little to establish either the adolescent's respect for or basic trust in the parent and goes far towards denying the adolescent an essential and universal criteria for successful social interaction — secrets. Any optimism the parent and teenager might have initially entertained with respect to converting the other to a position of right thinking will decrease at about the same rate as the level of frustration increases. The result is a double bind. The suicide attempter is much more a victim of the above process than the control adolescent.

TABLE 9-I

Percent of Experimental and Control Parents Using Selected Disciplinary Techniques (as Perceived by the Adolescent)

	Experimental Mothers (N=49)	Control Mothers (N=32)	Experimental Fathers (N=41)	Control Fathers (N=25)
1. Whipping	36% (18)	18% (6)	51% (21)	32% (8)
2. Spanking (Slapping)	48% (24)	37% (12)	48% (20)	40% (10)
3. Withholding Privileges	69% (34)	65% (21)	48% (20)	52% (13)
4. Withholding Approval or Affection	20% (10)	6% (2)	17% (7)	8% (2)
5. Holding Out Promises of Rewards	24% (12)	31% (10)	17% (7)	32% (8)
6. Talking Things Over, Discussing the Problem	63% (31)	75% (24)	31% (13)	40% (10)
7. Criticizing	61% (30)	28% (9)	36% (15)	28% (7)
8. Nagging	61% (30)	25% (8)	24% (10)	12% (3)
9. Yelling	77% (38)	34% (11)	53% (22)	20% (5)
10. Other (Sent to Bed Without Dinner, etc.)	10% (5)	3% (1)	4% (2)	4% (1)

TABLE 9-II

Rank Order of the Disciplinary Technique Which the Adolescents Perceived to be the Worst One

Experimental Adolescents (N=45)	Control Adolescents (N=31)
1. Withholding Privileges	1. Withholding Privileges
2. Whipping	2. Whipping
3. None*	3. Criticizing
4. Criticizing	4. Spanking, etc.
5. Nagging	5. Withholding Approval
6. Spanking, etc.	6. Yelling
7. Yelling	7. Other
8. Talking It Over, etc.	8. Nagging
9. Promising Rewards	9. Talking It Over, etc.
10. Withholding Approval	10. Promising Rewards
11. Other	

*The category of "none" is included here because it ranked so high among those listed by experimental adolescents. "None" must, for the time being, remain an ambiguous category. It remains unclear whether the suicide attempters meant by "none" that all disciplinary techniques were equally not bad or that they all were equally bad. Judging from a variety of other negative statements made by the suicide attempters regarding their parents during the interviews, the authors feel that there is greater support for the latter conclusion.

Parents, School, and Peers: Indicators of a Progressive Social Isolation

The extent of the adolescent's alienation from parents at the time of the suicide attempt is put into sharp relief by the following statistic. Of the 46 percent who reported their suicide attempt to others, 43 percent of these reported it to their parents while 57 percent of them reported it to persons other than parents. This is particularly significant when 88 percent of all suicide attempts occurred in the home, often with the parent(s) in the next room. Our findings point out that with respect to his family and school life, the adolescent suicide attempter is cut off from persons with whom he can discuss his problems. More important, he has lost access to that sector of society that could not only listen to his problems but that might also aid in their resolution.

In light of this, it is not surprising to find that 23 percent of the suicide attempters and 0 percent of the control group either agreed or strongly agreed that "There is no one to turn to when I need to talk to someone." Forty-six percent of the suicide attempters and 20 percent of the control group either agreed or strongly agreed that "One of the worst things about my troubles is that they always seem to be without a solution when I have them." Thirty-four percent of the suicide attempters and only 3 percent of the control group agreed or strongly agreed that "I feel that talking about my problems really doesn't get me any place." Fourteen percent of the suicide attempters and 30 percent of the control group agreed or strongly agreed that "No matter how bad things get in life they usually get better (*see* Table 9-III).

TABLE 9-III

The Suicide Attempters: Romance and the End of Hope

1. 36 percent of all cases were involved in the terminal stages of a romance.
2. 22 percent of all female suicide attempters were either pregnant or believed themselves to be pregnant as a result of the romance.
3. 100 percent of those in the terminal stages of a romance had a serious argument with their boyfriend or girlfriend immediately preceding the suicide attempt (many of these arguments followed or were followed by serious arguments with parents as well).
4. 100 percent of those involved in a romance had, by way of the romance, increased conflict with their parents, i.e. were disciplined for coming in late, spending too much time with the boyfriend or girlfriend; parents waited until the last minute to decide whether or not the adolescent might schedule a date, etc.
5. 82 percent of all cases were characterized by a reciprocal "flattening of affect" between the adolescent and his parent(s).
6. 36 percent of all cases were not enrolled in school at the time of the suicide attempt.

The Physician and the Suicide Attempt

A significant factor contributing to the escalation of problems for the suicide attempter is physical or mental illness in the family. In 48% of all cases, either the adolescent, parent, or sibling was treated for some form of mental illness or serious physical complaints within the last five years. Fifty-four percent of adolescent suicide attempters had been treated for some serious physical complaint and/or some mental disturbance (including previous suicide attempts) within the last five years; 32 percent had some serious physical complaint; 16 percent had some emotional disturbance; and 6 percent suffered both physical and mental disturbances. Thirty-six percent of the parents of adolescent suicide attempters had been treated for either a serious physical complaint or mental disturbance within the last five years (including four suicide attempts made by parents). In 14 percent of all cases, suicide attempters had a sibling or close relative other than parent living with them who had been treated for a serious physical complaint or mental disturbance within the past five years.

These illnesses and hospitalizations serve to seriously disrupt the usual composition and interaction of the family and add considerably to the problems faced by the adolescent, e.g. they may result in (a) his dropping out of school, (b) losing a parent from the household, often for the first time and for an extended period, (c) possibly losing a parent through death, or (d) his assuming a parental role of caring for the sick or for younger siblings and taking care of the household and/or family business.

In light of these problems, the importance of the adolescent's contact with his physician in the weeks and months preceding the attempt cannot be overestimated. Forty-six percent of all suicide attempters had such a contact, and, of course, all were seen by physicians immediately following the attempt. Twenty-six percent were previously seen under similar circumstances on the occasion of a prior suicide attempt. Only 59 percent of those who had previously attempted suicide were treated. The remainder were not seen by a physician and kept the event secret. The doctor's interest in and aid to the adolescent and his problems, above and beyond his success in dealing with the specific physical complaint, may in these cases mean the difference between life and death.

The authors recognize that it is beyond the scope of the physician in a hospital setting or in private practice to undertake to reconstruct the biography of his patient, or the beliefs or meanings it engenders, through lengthy interviews. However, we believe that short of these procedures, and without the insight one develops by way of constant contact with suicidal persons over a prolonged period of time, suicidal persons are not easily distinguished from the "normal" persons. Without exception, the suicide attempt, where it was a first attempt, came as a great surprise to both the parents and peers of the adolescent. The physicians of these adolescents were also caught off guard. There is no indication in any of the cases that they had given or received any advance warning. This is not surprising since there exists no convenient mechanical means of anticipating a suicide attempt. A good deal must be known in advance about the individual involved, and such information is sorely lacking in the routine contacts of everyday life. One thing mutually agreed upon by both the experimental and control groups was that secrets are an essential part of life, particularly in adolescence. In this respect the adolescent suicide attempter finds himself in a disadvantaged position.

The problems of the adolescent suicide attempters seen by our staff and viewed within the context of the aforementioned three-stage progression to social isolation fall broadly into five categories: parents, poverty, peers, broken romances, and pregnancy. All of these are, in fact, problems that one does not readily discuss with others who are in a position to help resolve them. By and large, an involvement or failure in these acts or situations brings with it the negative sanctions of society. In addition, by the time the adolescent makes an attempt, he has pretty well convinced himself that talking about your problems gets you nowhere. It should be added at this point that his past experiences consitute good reason for him to hold this view. Such an attitude does not represent a spontaneous or arbitrary opinion on his part. In short, the suicidal youth is not easily distinguished from others because his biography is not common knowledge. Those events that gave him sufficient good reason to live have been negated in the course of time and remain unknown. What is required is that the physician invest the time and effort needed to uncover a minimal amount of information regarding his patient, in excess of that necessary for a medical evaluation. Our study reveals that a high percentage of illness for which the suicide attempter sought a doctor's aid fell into the category of *functional physical complaints not given to specific diagnosis.*

In light of this and other findings, we feel that in many cases the adolescent may seek out the physician, not for his expertise in the healing arts, but because of the high prestige and esteem that the position of doctor occupies in our society and the potential for help implicit in such a position. The analogy of the doctor functioning as a secular priest in the social order is a common one. In brief, not only is the doctor's position unique in terms of providing the suicide attempter with ready access to what he may feel is a potential source of help when all others have failed, but the doctor is one of the few people in whom one is free to confide and to whom one is free to confess. This is a function of the objectivity, impartiality, confidentiality, and anonymity assured in the doctor–patient relationship. No less important to those seeking help is the presumption that the doctor holds an office in one of the most powerful existing agencies of help: science. The doctor has a moral obligation to use this privileged position to the best advantage of those seeking his services. Keeping in mind the ready availability of the information that he is in a position to elicit, as well as the experiences and attitudes held by the adolescent suicide attempter as outlined in this paper, the authors suggest that it would be helpful for the doctor to compile a thumbnail biographical sketch of his adolescent patients covering the areas indicated in Chapters 7 and 8.

It should be noted that some of the adolescent's problems listed in the author's study are unique to this group of adolescents, e.g. poverty, high rates of desertion and divorce, or geographical mobility. However, given that the nature of the problems experienced by the adolescent during the different stages will vary across class lines, they seem nevertheless to adhere in their formal aspects to the three-stage progression outlined earlier and to lead inevitably to the progressive isolation of the adolescent from any meaningful social relationships.

The authors cannot overemphasize that one cannot anticipate the potentially suicidal adolescent on the basis of how many problem areas are included in any one stage of the process. It is necessary, rather, to consider how any set of events in time relate to a previous set in the biography of the adolescent and in what manner and to what extent the gestalt has succeeded in isolating the adolescent from meaningful social relationships. An adolescent, as a member of a group whose biography is characterized by the above profile and who holds attitudes associated with such a profile, has, in the authors' opinion, a high probability of attempting suicide.

REFERENCES

1. Jacobziner, H.: Attempted suicides in adolescence. *Journal of the American Medical Association,* Vol. 191, January, 1965.
2. Shneidman, E., and Farberow, N.: *Clues to Suicide.* New York, McGraw-Hill, 1957.
3. Teicher, J.D., and Jacobs, J.: Adolescents who attempt suicide. *American Journal of Psychiatry, 122*(11), May, 1966.
4. Teicher, J.D., and Jacobs, J.: The suicidal adolescent. Read at the American Public Health Association Annual Meeting, Chicago, October, 1965.
5. Teicher, J.D., and Jacobs, J.: Adolescent suicide attempts: The culmination of a progressive social isolation. Read at the American Orthopsychiatry Association Annual Meeting, San Francisco, April, 1966.

Chapter 10

SUMMARY AND CONCLUSIONS

IF there is a leitmotif to the articles in this book, it is that suicide is best viewed as a conscious, rational act and that the would-be suicide has to convince himself of the moral correctness of taking his or her own life. In the case of those leaving suicide notes, an added effort is made to convince the survivors as well.

The recommendation is made to take into account the intentions, motives, and morals of suicides, in order to better understand suicide. It should be noted that if one leaves these features out of the sociological equation, one can (according to some schools of sociology) still be sociological. However, the author feels that in adopting this strategy, one is unlikely to gain a true sociological understanding of suicide or other social phenomena. One way to achieve this goal is through the application of a phenomenological approach to the study of suicide. Such an orientation is presented in several of the articles.

It has further been noted that people do not attempt suicide on impulse. Most have given the matter a good deal of prior thought. Nor do they decide that death is preferable to life. It seems rather that suicidal persons (like nonsuicidal persons) would prefer to go on living. The problem is that they have been unable to meet the minimum human requirement for such an undertaking, i.e. they have been unable (not withstanding their every effort) to establish and maintain reciprocal meaningful social relationships over time. Without succeeding in this, one comes to experience life not as full of ups and downs, but only downs.

With time, and under such circumstances, one experiences an end of hope.

This leads one to entertain the idea of suicide (suicidal ideation). Suicidal ideation, it is argued, may be like cigarette smoking — *dangerous to your health.* Certainly it is understood that way by most practitioners within the helping professions. The form that suicidal ideation must take to fit this model is noted in Chapters 3 and 4. On the other hand, suicidal ideation per se need not work to place one's life in jeopardy. In fact, entertained in another form, (as noted in Chapter 5) suicidal ideation may serve to prolong the life of the would-be suicide.

It has been argued throughout the book that suicide is not a form of mental illness, nor is it symptomatic of some other form of underlying mental illness. But what of cases of suicide among those diagnosed mentally ill, for example among manic depressives? Do these people attempt or succeed in suicide in some unconscious, irrational, or impulsive way? The study in Chapter 6 argues against accepting this view in some offhanded way on the basis of official statistics.

Finally, Chapters 7, 8, and 9 deal in different ways with adolescent suicide attempts. Chapter 7 deals with the role of progressive isolation in suicide attempts and the kinds of things that contribute to this state of affairs for adolescent suicide attempters. Chapter 8 deals with an analysis and critique of the role of broken homes in early childhood and whether or not it produces or predisposes one to depression or suicide in later life.

Lastly, in Chapter 9, we have considered the role of the physician as secular priest and how doctors are often consulted by potential suicides for nonmedical problems immediately preceding suicide attempts. Why physicians are not overly effective in suicide prevention during this cry-for-help period and how they might improve their effectiveness was considered in some detail in this paper.

In conclusion, the author hopes that these studies have provided the reader with a general framework from which to understand, relate to, and/or treat suicidal persons. If so, what seemed like a good idea in the beginning, will have proved to be one in the end.